LEAVING CLEVELAND

a fictional memoir

For San love, Izzy

"We never taste happiness in perfection, our most fortunate successes
are mixed with sadness." Pierre Corneille

print ISBN: 978-1-66788-843-9

ebook ISBN: 978-1-66788-844-6

Book Cover Photo by Steven H. Begleiter

First Edition

FOR MY FAMILY, WHOM I HOLD CLOSE TO MY HEART
AND WHO LIGHT UP MY WORLD.

KATE, MAKHESH & TIKA

In memory of my father, Jack, and mother, Ruth.
If character is judged by how one reacts to adversity, they are superheroes.
My beloved sister Melodie, whose name was chosen to celebrate
the first meeting of my parents in the Temple choir, who inspires me
every day and sadly left this earth way too early.

TABLE OF CONTENTS

LEAVING CLEVELAND

STEVEN H. BEGLEITER

CHAPTER 1

FELIX THE CAT

I wanted out of Cleveland. Immediately after college, I moved to Toronto, hoping to land a job as a news photographer, only to be told by the *Toronto Star* that I needed six months' residency in Canada before I could be hired. I should have known this. I headed back to the USA, driving southeast on Route 403, my Toyota Corolla hugging Lake Ontario to Niagara Falls, en route to Boston where I had a friend, Robert, who said I could crash on his couch until I found work. I had $500 in my pocket.

I drove straight through, from Toronto to Boston, without stopping. When I arrived in Boston, I met up with Robert who was living in an apartment near Harvard Square with his girlfriend, Ivey, and Felix, a semi-domesticated feral cat I was warned to avoid.

I had known Robert since I was 14. He had long blond hair, crystal blue eyes, and a swimmer's body. Soft-spoken, confident, and introspective, girls swooned over him, including Ivey who had moved from Finland to the States to live with him. He was everything I wanted to be. My mother would call it goy envy. Still, as opposite as Robert and I were, we connected. We both loved jazz and eventually formed a trio, with Robert on congas, our friend Alex on standup bass, and me on alto sax. We would jam in

Robert's attic for hours, smoking pot, and pretending it was the '50's, and we were the Coltrane trio. Robert's father, a lawyer, would sometimes tape-record our sessions and wait till we came downstairs to tell us how wonderful we sounded. His hipness freaked me out.

I spent two weeks in Boston looking for work, sleeping on a mattress on the floor, and avoiding Felix as best I could. Eventually I picked up some freelance photography work through the Associated Press, photographing "weather shots" while I waited to hear from a couple of newspapers about a staff position. It seemed there were no real jobs to be found. With my money running out, I took a job as a waiter at the Yankee Lobster in the Seafood district. I was feeling pretty low and thinking maybe I should head back to Ohio and work for my dad. He owned an outdoorsman store in East Cleveland, which never made any sense to me since he was not in the least interested in outdoor activities. He spent all of his days inside, working ten-hour days, seven days a week.

One night after work I arrived back at Robert's and he told me my sister Rachel had called. I hadn't spoken to her in months and wondered if it was bad news. I anxiously rang her back.

"Hi Rachel, what's up?" Her tone of voice told me nothing bad had happened. She said she had called to pitch me a proposition. "OK," I said.

"Sam, do you want to move to NYC and be my roommate?"

"Come again?" I said.

"My roommate Sherry is getting married and will be moving in with her fiancé in about a month. I can't afford the rent by myself, and Mom said you were sort of drifting."

"Drifting? Mom said I'm drifting. You need to tell her I am close, very close, to landing a job with *The Boston Globe*."

"The total rent is $800 and includes utilities. It's rent-controlled, in a great neighborhood, and has a doorman. For $400 dollars a month you'd be living in a posh Upper West Side apartment in Manhattan."

"Really? Well—just speaking hypothetically—if the job at the *Globe* did happen to fall through, how am I supposed to come up with the $400 a month? What would I do? It would take me a while to get a job and I'm not sure I could make the first month's rent?"

"I've thought about that. I spoke to my boyfriend Derek. He says he could hire you as a part-time laborer with his construction crew until you find some work."

"Wow, Rachel, you really have thought this thing through. And really, I appreciate your offer. I do. I'm just not sure NYC is a good place for me."

"Sam, you have no idea how exciting New York is. Imagine being a photographer here. I mean a real photographer! Derek is an artist. He could introduce you to the art scene. Who knows? Anything could happen."

I told my sister I would think it over and get back to her, that I needed to check on some things. I hung up the phone feeling dizzy.

Just then the door opened, and Robert walked in with his head down.

"Hey Sam, Ivey and I were wondering how long you wanted to stay with us?" I said nothing.

"I mean, not that we want to see you go or anything. We just want what's best for you," Robert said.

"What's best for me? I haven't got a clue what's best for me! OK? But fortunately, you and Ivey seem to know: My finding another place to live would be best for me."

"Hey, man, I didn't say that. It's just, well, if it were just me living here, I would say you can stay as long as you like. But Ivey, she wants a little more privacy."

Robert now managed to look me in the eye. I apologized. He had been generous, and he was right. It was time for me to go.

"OK. Understood. And, besides, man, I'm getting tired of smelling like fish and having your cat shadow me around the apartment when I get home!"

We both started laughing.

"You know I think it's time for me to move on and maybe the Big Apple is the remedy for my indecision blues."

Robert smiled and said, "We will miss you, man. Let me know when you've settled in. I'm definitely coming to visit."

"You're always welcome to stay with me, even if it's in a dumpster. But, hey Bro … a short visit."

Two days later I was back in my Corolla barreling west on the Massachusetts Turnpike.

CHAPTER 2

LUCY IN THE SKY
WITH DIAMONDS

Rachel and I had always gotten along. Although she was six years older, we had similar interests. We both aspired to be artists: she a painter; me, a photographer. We liked the same type of hippie music. We were both reasonably adventurous, though in truth she was much more so. I think what really bonded us was a drug experience. She got hold of some LSD from a boyfriend and offered me a tab. Our parents were out of town. I had never done that kind of drug but I trusted her. Her boyfriend had placed the tabs in two peanut butter cookies. At the count of three we both started eating the cookies. Then we waited for something to happen. Fifteen minutes. Half an hour. Nothing. A Bust. But then … we looked at each other. We started laughing. Before long the walls were undulating and Rachel was waving her arms rhythmically and saying she was a windmill. I was seeing rainbows tracing behind the movements of her arms like jet contrails. "It's getting weird," I told her. But Rachel assured me everything would be fine. "Let's go outside and walk around Shaker Lakes!" she said. We must have walked for hours, from our modest house in Cleveland Heights to the mansions in Shaker Heights. We talked about Nixon, Jackson Pollack, the Vietnam War, Baba Ram Dass, our favorite foods. I was listening to my heartbeat and to what seemed like thousands of singing birds. I didn't think about the time until I saw the long shadows and realized the whole day had elapsed. When we reached our house again it was dark.

Entering, we heard the phone ringing. Rachel ran to the kitchen to pick it up. "Hi Mom, how is the cruise?" As soon as I heard the "mom" word, I froze up and held my breath. "No. We're just hanging out. Everything is fine. How is Dad?" Rachel asked. She looked at me and mouthed, "Do you want to talk to Mom?" I waved my hands frantically and mouthed *Noooo*. "Mom, Sammy just took off to go to the bathroom, but I will fill him in. I love you too."

Rachel looked at me exasperated, "What's your problem?"

"My problem? My problem is I can barely speak a complete sentence. Mom would know I was high or something and cut her trip short to come home! How do you act so calm anyway? Aren't you still high?"

"Of course, but I'm in the moment, you know, 'be here now.'"

We raided the refrigerator and made baloney, Velveeta, and mayo on white bread sandwiches and ate like we were starving. I opened up a box of Ding Dongs and we devoured them. Feeling satiated, we went our separate ways; I into my room and she into hers. I stayed awake all night staring at the ceiling until the sun rose.

My thoughts raced as I steered from Highway 84 to 684. Boston in the rearview, New York looming ahead. I started feeling a bit nervous. I wasn't sure how to get onto the Tappan Zee Bridge. I pulled off the road and asked for directions from a cashier at a truck stop. I bought a Kit Kat and a Coke and got back into my car. As I approached the on-ramp, a young woman waved me down. I pulled over.

"Sorry to bother you but I need a lift. I can pay you," she said, breathing heavily.

"Which way are you going?" I asked.

"Towards New York," she said as she opened the door and jumped in. "Where are you going?"

She was petite and I did not see her as a threat. Besides, she was not unattractive, in the right light.

"The Upper West Side of New York, and you don't owe me anything," I said. I turned to rearrange my stuff on the back seat to make room for her bag.

"Can we get going," she said impatiently, looking out the rear window.

"What's the hurry? "I asked.

"Look. Here it is. The cops are after me. I was just being friendly to some truckers when the cops came into the shop."

"Why would the police care about that?"

She gave me a sharp look. "I was trying to turn a trick."

How stupid to pick up a hitchhiker! I mean, she could have a gun and knock me off and take everything I own. Come to New York and become a famous photographer, Rachel had said. Right! Come to New York and become a statistic!

"Do you usually find your Johns at truck stops?" I asked, trying to sound calm and worldly.

"I was supposed to meet my girlfriend there, but the bitch never showed. She was my ride home. I wasn't supposed to be there that long." She reached into her bag and rummaged.

Oh boy! This was it! She was looking for her gun!

She pulled out a sketchbook and said giggling, "Do you want to see my sketches? I have been told I'm a pretty good artist."

Relieved, I responded, "Sure." She started leafing through her book of illustrations of Demons and Satan. She had copied Hieronymus Bosch's *Garden of Earthly Delights*, the third panel. The one with all the horrific images of Hell. She looked at me. "What do you think?"

(What do I think? I think you're crazy and I think I'm crazy for allowing you to get into my car!)

"I think you are very talented and should consider art school," I said.

"Really," she responded, putting her hand on my thigh, and squeezing. "Look, I don't usually do this, but you are being so nice to me and all, if you pull off at the next exit, I'll give you a blow job."

I imagined pulling off into some discrete place in the woods and closing my eyes to relish the full intensity of an experience I had often fantasized about and getting hit in the head with a rock. I took her hand off my thigh, thanked her for her generous offer, and told her I had to get to an appointment in the city. I said I would drive her to her apartment, which she said was just north of the Tappan Zee Bridge.

"I'm really good at it. I could dig my nails deep into your back," she said.

"Ah, no thanks. I really have to go. Just tell me where you want to be dropped off."

I took her to her apartment. As she got out of my car she turned and said, "My girlfriend and I live in apartment 3C, if you ever pass this way, stop by and see us."

"OK, I will," I said.

I got back onto I-684, the span of the Tappan Zee Bridge straight ahead of me.

CHAPTER 3

CHANGE OF PLAN

I arrived in New York and found a metered parking space next to my new home, The Colorado, a 35-story doorman high-rise. I walked around to the front gold-trimmed revolving door and pushed through. Standing behind a long, curved Formica counter was a uniformed Hispanic man wearing a maroon captain's cap with shiny black trim.

"Can I help you?" he said.

"Ah, well yes. I am looking for Rachel Cohen. She lives here and is expecting me."

"Rachel Cohen is in 19K. I will ring her. You can wait till she comes down."

I sat in one of the lobby's cushioned chairs and looked around. The décor was beige with brown trim. A couple of Leroy Neiman knock-off paintings were hanging in gold metal frames. There was a tan chaise longue surrounded by two fake Areca Palm plants.

It had been a while since I'd seen my sister. She had moved to New York two years earlier, right after getting her MFA in painting from the Cleveland Institute of Art. She was determined to become a famous painter and for her New York was the place to make it happen. I looked up from the marble tiled floor and saw Rachel briskly walking toward me.

"Heyyy, you made it!" she said exuberantly.

I jumped out of my chair and gave her big hug, lifting her off the ground, which was easy since she was only 5 feet 4 inches.

"Where's your stuff?" she asked.

"In the car. I parked it around the corner." I looked at her, suddenly concerned. "Is it OK?"

"Is the car locked?" Rachel asked as if talking to an idiot.

"I don't remember. I think so."

"Jesus, Sam, you're not in Kansas anymore!"

My joy of seeing Rachel turned into panic and I ran out the door. I found my car and possessions intact.

"Everything still there?" Rachel said, walking up behind me.

"Looks like it. Can I get the doorman to help me? He must have some sort of dolly I can use. Maybe he could watch the car while I move things in?"

"His name is Jesus, and he won't help unless you give him some money. $20 should do," she said, pulling a $20 dollar bill from her blue jean's front pocket. I took the $20 and went inside to ask Jesus.

Not owning much makes moving easy. Within an hour, all my belongings were schlepped up to 19K and piled into my new room. The room was 10 steps long and 10 steps wide. Enough for a bed and a dresser. The floor was brown parquet, and the walls were white. What made the room was the view. A three-panel slide window facing south revealed mid-town Manhattan. There was a taller white apartment complex that blocked 50 percent of my view, but the panorama was still impressive. I couldn't believe my eyes. I had visited only once before, when I was 15, and I had vowed never to live in New York City.

My first visit to NYC was courtesy of High Mount Temple. I was recruited to work on a ship that was getting ready to travel to the Mediterranean Sea and anchor off the coast of Israel. The captain, Abie Nathan, a friend of the Beatles' John Lennon, had helped buy the ship and intended to use it as a base to broadcast unbiased news to the Jews and Arabs in the region, to promote peace. I mean, what could go wrong? Six underage, naïve Jewish teenagers from Cleveland working on a ship in the East Harbor of NYC. The entire time we docked in New York, we only left the ship once. Most of time we were painting the deck, cleaning the deck, making out on the deck. Our one moment of freedom, ironically, was a trip to shore to see an off-off-Broadway play *Jacque Brel is Alive and Well and Living in Paris*. After the play we walked back to the ship, my first glimpse of the NYC streets. All I could think was, how could anyone live in such a dirty, noisy, rundown place?

Our last night on the ship is forever branded in my memory. Abie told all of us to gather in the captain's quarters. When we arrived, he had us sit in a circle, crisscross applesauce. In his thick, baritone Israeli accent, he said "I want to thank you all for your hard work and sacrifice. I came to Israel in 1948 as an RAF pilot during the Israel/Arab War. I had a vision of bringing peace to the Middle East. I had witnessed too much destruction, despair, and oppression between the Jews and Arabs. All of you are making my vision turn into realty and I thank you."

Looking up at him from the floor he appeared to have a halo around his head. It was actually the dangling bare tungsten light behind him. He continued, "The reason I brought you here tonight is that I want to prove to you there is a higher power, and we are all one spirit." We looked at each other wondering what was going to happen next. "I am going to start with a simple demonstration. I will place thirty different objects in the center of your circle. One of you will leave the room. We will pick an object and when the person comes back, he or she will try to identify the object we chose. BUT REMEMBER, WE HAVE TO HOLD HANDS AND CONCENTRATE AND, MOST IMPORTANTLY, DO NOT LOOK AT

THE CHOSEN OBJECT!" Each time one of my shipmates picked the correct object a chill went up my spine, and my teenage nihilistic confidence waned. We were all in disbelief.

"Who wants a phone call?" Abie asked, looking around. "I do!" said Amy Feldman, one of my best friends. "Ok, we will all continue to hold hands and concentrate on Amy getting a phone call." We sat silently looking at each other in anticipation of experiencing something akin to the climax of a ghost story, waiting for what seemed like an eternity, beginning to think this is not going to happen. Abie broke the silence and whispered, "This does not always work but we must try and concentrate."

I started to fidget, losing circulation in my legs. I was ready to jump up and put an end to the charade when the phone rang. We collectively gasped. The phone kept ringing.

"Who wants to pick up the phone?" Abie asked. "I will," Danny Epstein blurted. His father was the son of the Rabbi at High Mount Temple and we all thought he had a direct connection to a higher being. Danny picked up the phone and put the receiver to his ear. I could see his face turn white and hear him mumbling "Uh-huh." Pushing his black-framed glasses up the bridge of his nose, he handed the phone to Amy Feldman who was shaking. "Who is this?" she asked cautiously. I watched her face go from a nervous smile to a blank zombie expression in about five seconds. Then she threw the receiver of the phone down as if it was on fire and turned to us with a blank stare. Speaking in a monotone voice, she said, "It was a man, but he wasn't sure why he was calling." I didn't sleep well that night and, for the first time in my young life, I started to shed my nihilist skin and cautiously started thinking about a higher spirit. Maybe it was that spirit that protected my father in the concentration camps. The six of us never talked about what happened that night but when we left the ship to head back to Cleveland, we were all changed.

CHAPTER 1

AN ENGLISHMAN
IN NEW YORK

Over the next few months, I got to know Rachel's English boyfriend, Derek, pretty well. He was an artist, but to make ends meet, he had a contracting business. He made his mark in the art world in the '60's by painting bold colors on large geometrical canvases. When the trends changed in the '70's his work wasn't in demand. He told me it was his English accent that got all the attention. He had trained himself to speak the Queen's English before he came to America because it sounded much better than his native Cockney. Gallery curators would invite him to private parties to impress their guests. He said he felt compelled to memorize some Shakespeare sonnets so as not to disappoint. That was then. Now Derek scrambled for contracts to demolish and renovate apartments. He stored his unsold art in his loft on the Lower East Side, waiting for the day when he would be rediscovered. Until then I could work on his wrecking crew.

On my own, I picked up a freelance job with the Associated Press as a "weather photographer," and so when I wasn't knocking down sheetrock for Derek, I was roaming the streets of New York looking for the Henri Cartier-Bresson decisive weather moment. On hot summer days I roamed the city streets searching for delinquent pubescents who burst open the fire hydrants to stay cool. With the sunlight behind them, I would snap their silhouettes distorted by a spray of water, creating the universal symbol of an urban heatwave. In the winter I would either head to Central Park and try to recreate the famous winter images by Andreas Feininger, or to the Rockefeller skating rink at night taking advantage of the skills I learned in college when photographing professional hockey for the Cleveland Barons, to the delight of my photo editors at the AP.

In a city of seven million, I was feeling very alone. Rachel and Derek would spend most of their time at his loft and when they were at the apartment they wanted privacy. I would find myself walking around the Upper West Side toward the Hudson River, wondering what I was doing in New York. I often stopped at the West End Bar for a beer, looking for someone to talk to. One evening I came back to the apartment and Rachel and Derek were sitting at the dining table. They looked happy, but when they saw me they got serious.

"Derek and I have decided to live together," Rachel announced.

My heart sank.

"OK." I tried to look upbeat. "But, uh, what am I going to do?" I said.

Rachel gave me a look of confusion before asking, "What do you mean 'What are you going to do'?"

"I mean, where am I going to live? I just moved here. I'm still trying to make rent."

"You, Sam, are going to stay here, and I am going to live in Derek's loft."

"But I can't afford the rent alone!" I replied.

"We will find you a roommate. I will not move until we do. In fact, I may already have a new roommate for you." My jaw dropped and seeing my disappointment Rachel looked at me crosswise, "I thought you would be happy for us?"

"I am. I'm sorry. I'm a jerk. I'm just not sure New York is the right place for me."

I felt left out.

"I think it is," Derek smiled, playing the older brother. "It just takes time to get your bearings. Don't forget, you're living in the center of the universe!"

I took a deep breath and began to calm down. I gave Rachel a hug and we held each other. "Mazel Tov!" I said. "I am happy for both of you. Really. I am."

CHAPTER 5

THE ROOMMATE

A week passed and I almost forgot that Rachel was moving out. I was on the Upper East Side knocking down walls with a sledgehammer when Derek came up to me and announced, "Well, I think it's all set. I just got off the phone with your sister and she said you'll have your new roommate by the first of September."

"What?" I said, trying not to lose my cool. "Don't I get to meet him first, to see if I even want the guy as my roommate?"

Derek put his hands up defensively.

"Rachel only told me that she has a friend who has a brother about your age who is looking for a place in Manhattan. I'm sure he's fine. Your sister wouldn't set you up with a bad roommate."

"So, I have no say?" I looked at Derek waiting for some response. He smiled.

"I guess not. It will be OK. According to your sister, he's studying psychology and comes from a good Long Island family."

"What's his name?" I asked.

"Howieeee," Derek said with his best Long Island accent.

As it turned out "Howie" was from Cedarhurst, Long Island, an affluent Jewish community. In public he fashioned himself the young Freud, with a thick black beard, wearing a tie and a vest with a pocket watch. In the apartment he transmogrified into a Hassid, stripped down to his white Fruit of the Loom T-shirt (stained under the arm pits), ankle-high sweatpants, and white socks. That was Howie.

For the newcomer, surviving New York is all about making rent. Derek employed me part-time but I needed another job. Going through *The Village Voice*, I saw an ad that read, "Sell over the phone. No experience needed. Good pay." I called the number, showed up for a job interview, and was hired. I was now a sweet-talking, sell-anything, clock-watching telephone solicitor. I was also getting very depressed. This was not why I came to New York.

My lifeline to the world had always been my camera. I was Diane Arbus, Irving Penn, Richard Avedon. Yet I was working as a telephone solicitor selling unwanted subscriptions of *Reader's Digest* to elderly women in living on Main Street in Kansas City. It paid the rent, but it was excruciating. Hour after hour, day after day, I watched the second hand of the clock slowly edging towards my liberation. Worse, I was good at the job! I almost always met my quota early.

After about three weeks, I was fired for using the phone to call friends around the country. Walking up Broadway to my apartment, newly unemployed, I pondered what to do next. I needed a job to pay my rent, but I wanted to get paid taking photos.

When I got home, I found a message on my answering machine. It was my friend Mark, who was free that night and wanted to get together. He said he had a proposition. Mark was also an aspiring photographer. We met at a bar called the West End, where I overheard him trashing some photographer he had worked for. Unsolicited, I decided to chime in.

"I hear she's a bitch to work for."

Mark gave me the "Who the fuck are you? look," before his face lit up, "You know her?" he asked.

"Ah, well, I've heard about her and how she treats her assistants."

"You heard right," Mark said. "She makes her assistants clean the toilets at the end of the day and she fires them if they look at her the wrong way."

"Wow that's rough. Why do people work for her?" (God, I thought. I really do talk like a hick from Ohio!)

"She's a famous fashion photographer. What photographer doesn't want to hang out with anemic models and bodybuilders?" he said sarcastically.

I extended my hand to Mark. "I'm Sam and looking for work as a photo assistant. Got any ideas?"

Raising his eyebrows he asked, "What do you know?"

"Um, I know the difference between an f-stop and shutter speed, and a little about strobe lighting."

"How little?" Mark asked.

"I know enough to fake it till I make it, "I said nervously.

"That'll do," he said.

I bought a round of drinks. He bought the next one. And the next. We talked small talk until, eventually, Mark got around to his "proposition."

It involved the photographer he was currently assisting.

"He is a great guy to work for, a bit of a space cadet, but generous."

"What's his name?"

"Well, I call him the White Rastafarian since he smokes a big spliff before he begins the day, one for lunch and, after the 12-hour workday, one more."

"Wow, how does he function? I mean, didn't you say he was a high-end commercial photographer?"

"He is. He bills about three to five grand a day for his higher-end clients. I've been working for him about a year and I'm beginning to burn out. I need a change. Hey, can you come to work with me tomorrow so I can introduce you?"

"Sure," I said, trying to contain my excitement.

"Great! I've got to go meet my wife. Here's the address. I'll meet you at 8 a.m."

"Cool!!! But why do you want me to meet him?"

"Because if he likes you, you can have my job," said Mark with a Cheshire Cat grin.

"What are you going to do?" I asked nervously.

"Me? I have an interview with a really famous photographer and if she hires me, I'm going to take that job."

"When do you find out?" I asked.

"In about two weeks. That will give me time to train you, if you get the job."

"OK," I said, trying to sound nonchalant. "I guess I'll see you tomorrow."

"Yep!" Mark said, flashing his bright white teeth again.

I soared out of the West End. I couldn't believe a chance encounter with a stranger could propel me in the direction of my dream. Of course, I had no idea if I would get the job but then, what did I have to lose? I mean, I had just lost my job selling the *Reader's Digest* to total strangers.

It was dusk and the streetlights were beginning to glow. New York City at its best. People swarming the sidewalks, weaving around each other, trying not to make eye contact—unless there was a physical attraction or a con. New Yorkers with their heads down and tourists with their heads up. Walking the streets of NYC was a game. You avoid contact and look ahead to the crosswalk, gauging whether to cross or not. The street strategy was to move as quickly as possible to get from point A to point B without stopping.

Entering my apartment building I ran into my neighbor Cindy, another starving wannabe artist living in a high rise waiting for her big break. Her dream was to be on Broadway. She also had the luxury of a Daddy who paid for everything.

I liked her, nonetheless. She was a Jersey Jewish girl who complained more than I did.

"Hi Cindy, what's new?"

"Oh, I just had an audition from hell. I waited three hours to be seen and then had two minutes to perform. It was just awful!"

"Well, there's always the next audition," I said encouragingly.

She lifted her eyebrows, turned toward the elevator doors, and started chewing her gum.

"I have sort of an audition tomorrow too," I said.

She gave me a bewildered look.

"I thought you took pictures."

The elevator door opened and we both got in.

"Well, I do take pictures. The audition is for a photo job."

"Hey, I need new headshots. Can we barter or something? I'm broke."

"Maybe ... if I get this job. Then I would have a place to shoot. What can you give me?"

She smiled as the doors opened. We happened to live on the same floor. She continued to smile at me and headed to her apartment.

"Good luck with the job interview," she said, as she unlocked her door and disappeared.

Cindy was very pretty but I was suspicious of dating a woman too dependent on their father's money. I felt more at ease with independent women. In part because of the strong independent women I grew up with.

This revelation became clear on my first and last date with a woman from Great Neck Long Island, Marci Greenblatt. Trying to impress her, I took her to Lincoln Center to see a ballet and then out for dinner at a restaurant nearby. I told her I was a photographer and she replied in a very serious tone, "Don't worry, if we get married you can work for my father. He owns a button factory."

Growing up poor and Jewish in the suburbs of Cleveland, and attending temple in an affluent neighborhood, may have been the cause. Every Sunday morning as a child I was woken abruptly with my mother shouting, "Wake up and get dressed, you're going to be late for Temple!" In Temple, I would hear all the wealthy Jewish kids brag about their new toys, ski vacations, and trips to Europe. I would count the minutes in anticipation of my mother picking us up and driving to the Howard Johnson's restaurant across from Severance Hall, where the Cleveland Orchestra performed.

Rachel and I would order the Black Cow, root beer, and vanilla ice cream. The whole time Rachel would lament about how small our house was and how we should move to a bigger house in Shaker Heights. As I sucked at my straw to get the last of my Black Cow, Rachel continued to whine. I could see my Mom's face turn beet red, trying to look earnest, while chain smoking her Virginia Slims and avoiding another public display of anger.

My mother had a rough start in life. At the age of six she nearly died in a fire that started when she and her friend were playing with matches in the closet. Her body was severely burned and she underwent extensive treatments and skin grafts, spending more than a year in the hospital. The doctors were uncertain whether she would survive. The burns left visible scars on her neck and chest, but the emotional scars and the experience of being ostracized as a child and young adult because of the disfigurement hurt her the most. I often wondered if that trauma was the reason for her sharp temper and, paradoxically, her attraction to my father who was traumatized in the concentration camps. When they met, he barely spoke a word of English and was "a poor immigrant" according to my maternal grandmother, who would add, "at least he is Jewish."

Walking into my apartment, I discovered Howie sitting on the couch, watching a cable show where the hostess wears a bikini and talks about the porn industry. Howie's father was a therapist and Howie had decided to follow in his father's footsteps. He was getting his master's in psychology at Columbia and had already identified 115 percent of his phobias.

"Hey Howie, what are you doing?"

"Nothing. Just waiting for a call."

"A call from…" I paused, hoping he'd fill in the blank. He did not.

He said nothing. So I gave him my news. "I might get a job tomorrow."

"That's great," he said, continuing to stare at the TV.

"Well, I'm going to bed early. Got a big interview tomorrow. See ya."

"OK."

Howie's eyes were bloodshot. He was stoned again.

I entered my 10' × 10' × 8' white room and closed the door. I stared out my window looking south toward Lincoln Center. I had two pieces of furniture, my futon mattress and a dresser that I found in a dumpster on the Upper East Side. I think it might have been a Chippendale, made of solid mahogany.

On top of the dresser were some magazines. I randomly pulled down an old *National Geographic* and plopped my body on the futon. I found an article about cockroaches. I knew all about cockroaches, as any New Yorker does. The article taught me obscure facts about these prehistoric creatures. Indeed, I was feeling some empathy for these pesky and persistent insects. They were long-term conquerors that would outlive the human race. As I read, my eyesight started blurring and I could feel sleep approaching. Suddenly I heard tiny tapping noises about my head. I looked up and there was a cockroach, still as night, looking down at me. Had he been reading about his family? I closed the magazine and, with the quickness of a gunslinger, BAM! I smashed the little sucker. Yuck. It was now embedded on the cover of the *National Geographic*. Fame had arrived.

The loud sound startled my roommate and he poked his head in my door.

"What's going down, man?" he exclaimed.

I showed him the cover of the magazine. He studied it for quite a while before announcing, "Wow, NG is now doing 3D covers."

The next morning my alarm clock sounded at 6 AM. I was about to hit the snooze button and settle in for another hour or so when I realized: THE JOB INTERVIEW. I forced my eyes to focus on the stucco white ceiling. I stood up and looked down at the futon bed and gazed at the gut stain the cockroach had left on the wall. Opening my bedroom door, I saw Howie asleep on the couch. He was snoring loudly.

I jumped into the shower, thinking about the upcoming interview. I knew nothing about commercial photography. I wanted to be a street photographer, capturing decisive moments, revealing truths, telling visual stories about the human condition. I did not want to create images to sell stuff people didn't want or need. Then again, some of the most creative images I knew were ones I had seen in ads. I mean, Bert Stern was only 20 when he was flown to Egypt to photograph the great Pyramids with a Martini glass in the foreground. All to sell Vodka. And Vodka was enjoyed around the world. It gave pleasure. Soothed pain. Stern's iconic images sold products that benefitted society. My guilt at the thought of contributing to the decline of Western Civilization washed away in the suds as my shower ended abruptly with a loud knock on the door.

"You almost done? I have to get to class," Howie yelled.

"Yep. I got an interview in an hour. I'll be right out," I said. I wrapped a towel around my wet body and stepped out of the steamy room.

Howie was already in the kitchen making a pot of coffee.

"It's all yours," I said in an upbeat voice.

Walking into my room, I looked into the closet. What to wear? The White Rastafarian would probably prefer if I had dreadlocks and a beard but there was no time for that. I pulled out a pair of faded Levi jeans and a blue button-down work shirt. I decided to take a risk and put a gold stud earing on.

I looked in the mirror and started to feel confident. I was definitely moving in the right direction. I made some breakfast, had a little coffee, and headed out the door.

CHAPTER 6

THE WHITE
RASTAFARIAN

The Upper West Side of Manhattan on an early Monday morning is always bustling, as it is throughout the day. The difference is, in the morning, the faces look more expectant, as if something big is going to happen. Not that anybody looks at anyone else. But the crowd moves with a purpose. For me that street dance was a bit lighter knowing that I could end the day with a job.

I dropped my subway token into the turnstile and pushed my way underground. The plan was to take the Local 3 train to Times Square, transfer to the crosstown, and end up on 23rd and Park. I squeezed my body onto the train and, trying not to look anyone in the face, I stared at a black and white photo of Mayor Ed Koch looking like a friendly Dopey from Sleeping Beauty. Above his bald head was the tagline: "Graffiti is a Crime." I looked out the window. A graffiti-covered train rocketed by on the other track.

It was rush hour and every conceivable business fashion combo was on display: ties with jackets, T-shirts with jeans, heels with dresses, heels with pants and Jackie O sunglasses, red converse low tops with black leather coats, Ferragamo suits with sneakers. The train lurched. I checked my watch and saw I still had plenty of time in the event the train stopped dead in the middle of the tunnel. It kept moving and I was soon at my destination. I pushed out to the platform and up the steps to the fresh air of the street. I looked around to get my orientation. The big clock on the MetLife building was staring at me. I headed north toward 27th Street and Park Avenue South.

Ahead I saw Mark. He looked surprised to see me.

"I didn't think you'd remember our appointment!" he said in what I took to be a sarcastic tone.

"I'm dependability incarnate," I said.

He led me into a building on Park Avenue South and I followed him down a short and vacant hallway to the elevator. I looked around the hallway and could tell that this used to be a grand building. Now it was a bit rundown but still, with ornate plaster crown molding and marble floors, revealed a glorious past. The high ceilings were from a time when style preceded function and costs.

The elevator arrived and Mark and I stepped in.

"It's awfully quiet around here in the morning," I said.

Looking at the doors in front of us, Mark responded, "There are four stories in this building, and they are all occupied by Johnny's people."

"Who's Johnny?" I asked.

"I never did give you his name, did I?" Mark said.

"Nope," I said.

"Johnny Strand the photo man," Mark recited rhythmically, as the door opened onto the third floor.

We stepped into a dark and quiet room. Mark flipped the light switch. Everything was white: walls, floor, ceiling. I looked around and saw all the tools of a photo studio: strobe packs, lights, seamless paper neatly vertically packed in a rainbow of colors. There was a large box about 4 feet by 6 feet supported by four metal rods on wheels. I had never seen that before and I asked Mark what it was.

"I made that with Johnny last winter. It's a giant light bank. It holds 4 strobe heads and puts out 10,000-watt seconds of light. It's great for photographing people from head to toe and yields about f64."

This was a foreign language to me, but I put on a knowing gesture and exclaimed how incredible it was.

"Yea. It's become the major light source in most of our shoots now," Mark responded.

"So, when does Johnny arrive? "I asked, walking toward the back of the studio where there was a full kitchen.

"It all depends. He has a shoot this afternoon, so depending on how late he stayed out, I would say around one. That's why I wanted us to arrive early, to give me a chance to show you around."

I studied the kitchen. It was right out of one of those high-end kitchen magazines with all the high-end appliances.

"Does he like to cook?" I asked.

"No way! He likes to order in. Or if his wife's around, they go out," Mark said laughing.

"Then why the fancy kitchen?" I asked.

"For his clients. He has a few food accounts and this is where they prep the food."

"What food accounts?" I asked, immediately sorry I sounded so nosy.

"Right now, Arby's, though he's hoping to land McDonald's."

I walked past the kitchen and down a long hallway. I could smell a darkroom. I knew the Dektol odor from my days of working in the darkroom in college where I would spend hours breathing in the chemicals trying to make the perfect print. I never used the prescribed tongs when processing the light-sensitive paper in and out of the photographic chemistry. I would submerge my hands into the developer, pull out the print at just the right moment, and drop it into the acetic acid stop bath and into the fix bath, rocking the trays as if that would speed up the process. It was magical. "Can I check out the darkroom?" I yelled down the hall.

My first darkroom was modest. I constructed it in the basement of our Cleveland Heights home. I was only 14, and not having any parental supervision worked to my advantage. I built it in the back of the basement where there was a small storage room with a door I could close to keep the light out. It also had shelves to place my developing trays and an enlarger. There was no plumbing in the converted closet. I would load the film onto the metal reels and place them into the light tight film tank. Once I knew the top of the tank was securely screwed on, I would step out into the light and process my film in the rusted sink next to the washer and pray for good results. Most of the time, the photo spirits were on my side.

This was the place where I would spend hours being an alchemist. It was my escape room from the bullies who would pick on me because I was Jewish; it was my escape room when my mother and father would get into an argument and start yelling about money, not spending enough time with us, or just releasing their pain. The unbearable noise would stop when the front door slammed, and I could hear my mother crying.

Rachel's escape was the sunroom on the second floor. She would close the door to the sunroom and brush paint on canvases. I would close the door to the darkroom, get stoned and process film and make prints.

"Sure. Just don't touch anything, I'll be right there." I waited till Mark joined me and he slid the pocket door open. It was a small darkroom but had all the right stuff: an enlarger that could hold 4- by 5-inch negatives and an easel big enough to make 20- by 24-inch prints, large plastic trays, even a venting system that sucked the toxic fumes out of the room.

"Now this is exciting!" I gushed.

"Sort of, I guess, if you like the smell of chemicals and enjoy the dark. I spend a little too much time in here to enjoy it. Do you see that giant stainless-steel box?"

"Yep," I responded.

"That holds up to 24 rolls of 120 film."

"You mean you process that many rolls at a time?"

"Sometimes two to three times a day. Once you learn the system, it's not so bad. Just remember," Mark said with a devilish smirk, "there's about five grand riding on that film and if you fuck up, it's ... not good. Still interested in the job?"

I nodded.

"Great, cause I really want out and I have an opportunity to work with this certain celebrity photographer, but I have to move fast before she finds someone else."

"Who is it?" I asked with genuine curiosity.

"Alright," Mark said and with his big Cheshire Cat grin he proudly announced, "Isadora Teivel."

"No shit? As in *Vinyl Magazine*? As in rock stars in the buff?"

"She is kinky! And impossible to work with. She goes through assistants like my uncle Aiden goes through scotch."

"Are you sure you want to work with her," I joked.

"Of course, I want to work with her. If I survive a year, my career is made."

"And maybe after a year or so when you move on, you'll call me to take your place again?"

"Maybe. First, let's see if you can take my place this time. Tell me what you know about studio photography."

I looked at Mark with a blank stare. He looked back at me with what looked like concern.

"Well," I said finally, knowing I had to say something, "I got my degree in photojournalism and ... and we did some studio setups. And I just learned how to work a light meter at another gig. I'm a quick learner. My motto is fake it till I make it!"

Mark was shaking his head.

"I really need to move on from here and I really, really want this new gig. So OK. Let me give you a rundown of the studio and tell you about your new potential boss. Just promise me one thing."

"Sure," I said.

"Fake it long enough for me to make it with Isadora Teivel. Let's start with the strobe lights."

"OK," I said.

"Johnny likes to use this giant soft box, which I made by the way. It has 6 strobe heads in the back and they all connect to these 2,400-watt second Speedatron packs, so when you do the math, you can see you have a lot of power."

My head was feeling a bit light and Mark's voice was fading as he described all the technical stuff. I began to wonder whether I was in over my head when I heard Mark say, "It can KILL YOU if you don't do it right." I snapped out my daze.

"What?"

"The strobes can electrocute you if you don't plug them in properly. They can arc!" he said seriously.

"Arc? What does that mean?" I asked.

"It means if they are not plugged in correctly, you die! So, you better stay focused. GOT IT?"

"Sorry. Go on. I was just a bit overwhelmed."

Mark was getting angry.

"Look. It's not rocket science. It is just common sense but you need to pay attention because I am only going to tell you once! Do you want this job?"

"I really do. Sorry. Let's get back to the strobes."

Mark went on to explain power ratios, light bank adjustments, the light meter. My head started spinning again. He showed me how, for product photography, he jerry-rigged a Plexiglas tabletop and placed strobe lights to illuminate the glass. It was quite ingenious, I thought. It seemed that all the lighting contraptions were self-made and original. My excitement started to overcome my fear.

At this moment I heard the elevator door open and into the room walked Johnny Strand the Photo Man. He was thin and stood about 5 feet 6 inches, with shoulder-length black curly hair, a full black beard, and round wire-rim glasses.

"Hey Mark, what's happening? "Johnny said, looking at me.

"Hey Johnny, this is Sam. He's also a photo assistant and he wanted to check out where I work and get a chance to meet you."

"That's right," I jumped in. "I've heard so many cool things about you and the work you do through Mark, I had to come down and meet you." I said, realizing I may have come on too strong.

"Well, I'm not sure what Mark told you, but it's cool," Johnny said with a smile.

I walked up to him and shook his hand. I saw that his eyes were bloodshot, and he smelled of Jasmine, which I took to be his effort to cover up the scent of pot. He had obviously smoked that morning. He had a warm and happy demeanor.

"So, are you from the Big Apple?" he asked.

"No, I'm from Ohio. I moved here after graduating from college."

"Which college?" he asked in a serious voice.

"The one where students are used as target practice, Kent State." I said sarcastically.

He looked me in the eye and sang, "Four dead in Ohiooo." Looking at me wide-eyed he asked, "Were you there?"

"No. I arrived on campus ten years after the fact, but I did get arrested and was even pepper-gassed by the National Guard." I said, trying to impress Johnny with my civil disobedience.

"What a bummer," he said, shaking his head. "Well, it was nice to meet you Sam. I hope to see you again." He turned to Mark. "We have a busy day man so let's have our morning meeting."

Mark looked at me and then at Johnny.

"Ah … Johnny," he said. "Sam wanted to stay the day and watch what we do and help out. At no cost."

A silence ensued.

Johnny looked at me and then at Mark. After a long pause he said, "Well, I suppose he can hang as long as he doesn't get in the way."

Yes! I thought to myself. "I'm in the door." Stay cool and DO NOT SCREWUP.

We sat around a round oak table and Johnny explained the day's agenda.

Although he looked stoned, when he talked about work he was serious as if he were planning a battle strategy. Concise and directorial.

"We have to set up the big light to test for a hair shot we are doing tomorrow. The client is Ogilvy, and the model is Heidi Starr. She is a bit of prima donna and I hear she can be cold as ice. The art director will be on board to help her warm up. I heard they might be sleeping together, so we'll see. Here's the AD's layout."

Johnny placed a piece of paper on the table with a hand drawing of a woman's profile with a big smile.

"That's pretty crude," said Mark.

"It was probably drawn by one of my dad's minions at the agency," Johnny said.

It turned out that Johnny's dad, Kirk, was a well-known and respected art director in the advertising world. He was Jewish and had emigrated from Germany just before Hitler had come to power. Kirk had attended the famous Bauhaus in Berlin where he was studying to be an illustrator. He met his wife there. She was studying to be a painter. The two landed in NYC in 1933, and Kirk got his first job as a copy and paste artist at an ad agency, eventually working his way up to senior art director at the infamous Lois Pitts Gershon. George Lois was well known in the industry for the insane antics he devised to garnish big accounts. Kirk, as talented as he was, did not have the tough personality needed to rise to the top of the industry, but as I learned later, he was happy enough to just create.

"So, in addition to the big light bank, we need a hair light. We are going to shoot with the Hassi and the 150 mm. We're shooting her on white so light the background. While you set up, I'm going upstairs to see how Ong is doing." Johnny got up and went into the elevator.

"Who's Ong?" I asked Mark.

"A piece of work!" said Mark. "Johnny's girl. She was born in Thailand and migrated to the USA with her parents in the '50's. She is gorgeous and a real princess. Johnny worships her and she takes full advantage of his generosity. If you stick around, you'll see what I mean. Let's set up the shot. I think Johnny likes you. So, watch and listen. I really want to move on."

Mark set up the big light bank and we both set up the 9-foot white seamless. Seemed easy enough. Then he pulled out the camera and my stomach knotted up. He detected my anxiety and, looking at me, said, "It's easier than it looks."

"I didn't even know they still made those cameras," I said. "I mean, I thought he was going to use the medium format camera?"

"Yea, me too. But he wants to start with the large format. I think he just wants to confuse the client because I have never seen him photograph a model with this camera."

"Maybe he wants to be like Irving Penn," I said.

Mark looked at me.

"Do you know how to load and work one these cameras?"

"No," I replied sheepishly.

"Well, this is a little more complicated but all you have to know is how to load and process the 4 by 5 film."

"OK," I said, feeling anything but OK.

"It looks like you have a lot of homework to do," Mark said. "But let's just try to survive today."

Mark spent the next half hour showing me the intricate ritual of loading this dinosaur of a camera. When he finished his lesson, he told me he was leaving me alone in the darkroom and I was to load all ten film holders. If I missed even one of them, he said, I was fired.

"Don't I need to be hired first?" I said.

Alone in the eerie light of the room, I looked at all the foreign objects and thought to myself, "Do I even want this job?" And then I thought about selling subscriptions over the phone.

I turned off the light and systematically loaded all the film. I am not sure how long it took, but when I was finished, I closed my eyes and turned on the lights. Slowly opening my eyes, I looked at the table to see if any film sheets had been left on the table. Fortunately, the table was void of any 4 x 5-inch film sheets. I slid open the door and saw Johnny and Mark sitting at the table.

They both turned around and stared at me.

"Here are ten sheets of film ready to be exposed," I said.

"Bring them here and we will inspect them," Johnny said, sounding like anything but a stoner.

I placed the film holders on the large oak table and Mark divided them to keep five for himself and five for Johnny.

"So," Johnny said to me as he examined my work, "Mark tells me he may have a better gig."

I played dumb. To divert the focus on me I said, "How did I do? I mean, was the film loaded correctly?"

"So far, so good "Johnny said. "Can you spend the week working here to see how we get along? I can't pay you now but you will get free lunch."

My heart racing, I pulled out my date book and leafed through the week.

"I have a couple of appointments ... but I think I can change them. Sure, I can spend the week here."

"Come sit. I want to learn more about you," Johnny said, pulling out a chair for me. "Tell me why you want to be a professional photographer?"

"Well, it started when I was around 14 and a friend, Dave Lindsey, introduced me to the darkroom. He played a trick on me and told me to put the photographic paper under the enlarger and expose the negative for 5 seconds, then place the light-sensitive paper under my shirt and run outside to expose the paper to the sun for only two seconds, cover it with my shirt and run back to the darkroom to process the paper in the chemistry. That was how I would make my first print."

At this point Johnny looked at me as if hoping I hadn't really told him that.

"Of course, the paper always came out black and my friend, after making fun of me, explained the correct way to make a print. And I was hooked. I decided to become a professional photographer. So, I signed up to be the photographer of the high school yearbook, went to college and was the staff newspaper photographer/editor and yearbook editor, got my degree in photojournalism and moved to New York to become famous."

"OK," Johnny said. "You won't become famous working for me. You won't earn a lot of money. The hours are long but the lunches are free. It can get pretty intense and you will have a lot of responsibility. Still interested?"

"It sounds absolutely great!" I said, trying to be funny.

"Well, let's see how this week goes. Mark likes you and thinks you can handle the job, plus he really wants out, which I don't understand but I need someone to take his position. If you last till Friday and all goes well, you can have the job. I like you and for some reason you remind me of me when I was your age. Are you Jewish?"

Johnny asked this with a Yiddish accent.

"Of course. Aren't all the great artists in New York Jewish?" I said.

Johnny laughed. "I think you will fit in. Mark doesn't get the Jewish humor, being a goy and all. But he is loyal and a good friend. Let's see how it goes. By the way, all the film was loaded correctly."

"So, what do I do first?" I asked.

"You see that mop and bucket over there by the bathroom..."

CHAPTER 7

I'M 'ENRY THE EIGHTH I AM

Everything Johnny said about the job proved true. Long hours, demanding clients, and a lot of unwarranted despair. My day started at 8. Johnny would walk in at 8:30 with blood-shot eyes, smelling of Jasmine, humming some Reggae tune and looking very happy. By lunchtime his glow was gone and in need of replenishment. Our lunch orders went out at noon to the deli downstairs. Johnny would absent himself and reappear an hour later just as the sandwiches arrived, his glow back. That's when Jenny, his rep, would arrive and join us and we'd sit as a team around the oak table and eat.

"Hey Johnny, how's it going?" Jenny would ask. She was slender, mousy brown hair, a beauty mark on her right cheek, and always dressed in a tight-fitting button-down shirt tucked into a long black skirt, which highlighted her narrow waist. She'd have on her signature scarf, always very colorful, meticulously tied around her neck. She was from Patterson, New Jersey, and had a thick Jersey accent.

On my first day at the oak table, Johnny asked her, "Any news about the Burger King account?"

She smiled and said, "It's between you and Tom Brody, but the art buyer said she liked the fact that you shoot other things besides food. I think you need to set up a test shoot of something with food that I can take over to her by the end of the week."

"Like what?" Johnny responded, his mellowness unmellowing.

"I don't know. You're the creative. You come up with something," Jenny said.

Johnny put his head down on the table like a child taking an afternoon nap in school. For five minutes we just stared at him. Suddenly he raised his right hand with his forefinger pointing to the ceiling.

"Let's photograph Henry the Eighth eating ice cream."

"Genius!" Jenny exclaimed. "That will combine your talent with people and food. Who can we get to play Henry?"

"Get the Funny Face catalog," Johnny commanded. "They owe us a favor and I think there are few models who will want to do this."

Jenny pulled out the catalog and Johnny flipped through its pages. After about ten minutes he slammed his fingers on a headshot and declared, "Tom Lang, he's perfect—belly, beard and all. I will get Ong to style it. Call Barbara and see if she's available to help."

The studio was instantly abuzz. Jenny was on the phone convincing Barbara, a food stylist, that doing this photo test would help her career. Johnny was on his way to the elevator, turning back to us, he announced, "I'll recruit Ong."

Jenny got off the phone and looked at me.

"We are on! We got the model. We got the food stylist. And now we cross our fingers and hope Johnny convinces Ong to do him a favor."

"What's she like?" I asked.

"Who?"

"Ong."

38

"Johnny met her about five years ago and it was love at first bite. She moved into his apartment the next day."

"So why wouldn't she do him a favor?" I asked.

"Because she is about money and is not into doing favors unless there is money involved."

"But still."

"Because she is Ong!" Jenny said coldly.

At that moment the elevator door opened and in walked Johnny and Ong. He had fetched her from their apartment, which was a floor above the studio. She had long black hair and a perfect petite body.

She was whining.

"But I have a busy week and finding a Henry the Eighth outfit will take time."

"Come on Ong," Johnny pleaded. "Please, please, please, babe. Do this for me."

"And what will you do for me?" Ong asked.

Johnny looked suddenly miserable.

"I don't know. Something from Bergdorf's. You can pick it out."

"When do you want to do the shoot?" she asked, looking victorious.

Johnny looked at Jenny. "How is your search going with the talent?"

Jenny grinned. "We're all set! We can shoot as early as Friday."

A calm came over Ong's face.

"Anything?" she purred.

Johnny nodded.

Ong smiled, turned and walked to the elevator. All was silent until she got in and the door closed.

Jenny laughed and looked at Johnny.

"I just hope we get the Burger King account so you can actually pay for her shopping spree."

The next day I was setting up the lighting and running a film test. Joe, an old friend of Johnny's, was the stand in for Henry the Eighth. Ong had borrowed an elaborate Tudor costume from Props Unlimited: silk and satin crimson-colored doublet, rich purple velvet coat with white fur trim, ornate Tudor hat, silk stockings. In addition, there was a treasure box filled with fake jewels and rings. I looked over to Joe and asked how she managed to borrow all this.

He looked and me. "I shouldn't be telling you this but since you work for Johnny, I guess it's OK.

It's less 'borrowed' and more 'trade.'"

"Yea?" I said. "What do they trade?"

"White powder," Joe said, raising his eyebrows.

"I'm sorry, Joe," I said. "I'm new to this. White powder?"

"You know, man, blow, snow, toot, coke. The owner of the Prop place is really hooked, so Ong has a 'friend' who supplies her with what she wants. Ong is a slippery one. I think she may be sleeping with the dealer, but I don't have the heart to tell Johnny.

This is our secret, OK?" Joe said with a serious look.

"Is Johnny into coke?" I asked.

Joe frowned. "He uses it when he needs that extra kick but he mostly smokes weed. It sort of balances out."

At that moment the elevator door opened and in walked Johnny. I looked at him in a whole new light. His mood swings made sense.

Smiling, he walked toward Joe and gave him a big hug.

"How's it going, man? Haven't seen you in quite a while," he said.

"I've been around," Joe said. "Busy working for a new cable TV company. Not sure it will go anywhere but they're teaching me how to install the wires and stuff. Nothing exciting. Hey, but today I am The King. Nobody can take that away from me!"

"You want to come upstairs for a bit? I want to share something with you," Johnny asked him, and then he turned to me. "Sam, how is the set up going?"

"Just fine," I said. "I have the seamless down and secure, lights are up. Just have to do some metering and organizing."

"Good. Joe and I are going upstairs for a while. Finish up so we can do a test shoot and get the film to the lab before 4."

"Sounds good," I said.

They came back down about 20 minutes later red-eyed and laughing and reeking of weed.

"Are you ready for your coronation?" Johnny asked.

"Not yet. Where's my queen?" Joe mugged.

"No queen," Johnny said. "Remember, you chopped her head off last week."

"Oh right, I forgot. By the way, do you have anything to eat? Like a drumstick?"

"What, now you're a method actor!" Johnny laughed. "Don't overdo the Henry the Eighth thing."

"No, man. I'm really hungry," Joe said.

"After the shoot we'll do lunch," Johnny said. "Go to the dressing room and dress up."

He turned to me.

"So, we're all set?"

"Yep. The lights are set and metered. Your Hassi is on the tripod and synched and ready for a Polaroid."

"Great. Why don't you stand in while Joe is getting dressed."

"I get to wear the hat?"

"You bet. You can even hold the ice cream cone."

So, I put on the Tudor hat, stood on my mark, and took a big bite out of the ice cream. POOF! Johnny took a Polaroid. We waited patiently for 60 seconds, and I watched Johnny peel apart the film and look at it.

"Close, but we have to crank up the background. It's not white enough. Double the power on the strobe packs and bring it up to f/22. What reading are you on?"

"F/16."

"OK. Then the background definitely needs to be pumped up to f/22."

He took another Polaroid. He waited. He checked it.

"Perfect!" he announced.

At that moment Joe came out of the dressing room looking nothing like King Henry the Eighth. Johnny sized him up.

"Sorry, Joe. There's been a usurpation. Sam here is our Henry the Eighth."

I thought this was funny, but glancing at Joe, I swear I detected a murderous glint in his eyes. *Jesus!* I thought. He knows this is all make-believe, right?

With Joe glaring, Johnny directed me to the spot, and he shot a roll of film.

"It's a wrap!" he said when he was finished, adding, "Sam, take this roll to the lab, do a clip test at a ¼ push, have Baboo judge it, and run the rest of the film, to be delivered first thing in the morning."

It always amazed me that no matter how stoned Johnny got, when it came to work, he performed like a battlefield general. Clear-headed, direct and driven. I knew I would learn a lot from him.

I walked out into the warm Manhattan evening and strolled down Park Avenue South toward the lab. I was feeling good. I was in the Big

Apple with a job in a real photography studio. I was so preoccupied with my happy thoughts that I passed the lab at 19th and Broadway. Turning back, I found it and dropped off the film with Baboo. I gave him Johnny's instructions. Back outside, I jumped on the IRT 123 north and headed back to my apartment.

The next morning I was at Johnny's studio at 8 AM sharp, and as I entered, I was greeted by a hum of excitement.

Barbara, the food stylist, had her tools spread out on the kitchen counter. She was explaining to Johnny how she was going to keep the ice cream from melting on the set. Anya, the hair and makeup artist, had her arm around a guy I didn't know and they were walking toward the dressing room. I asked Jenny who he was, and she told me he was the actor from the Funny Face model agency. *That was odd*, I thought. The guy looked nothing like the picture in the Funny Face catalogue. Anya and he obviously knew each other and were reminiscing about prior gigs. Just then the elevator door opened and in walked a delivery boy with coffee and donuts.

I grabbed a donut and toured the studio, making sure everything was ready for the shoot. The power pack ready lights were glowing; the camera sat securely on the tripod stand with the Polaroid back revealing the white paper tab, ready to pull for the first test shot; a cart next to it held three loaded Hasselblad film backs, all numbered, and an extra pack of Polaroid. The white seamless background was securely taped to the white cement floor and black tape arranged in the letter X marked the spot where the model was to stand. Everything seemed in place.

Johnny was in a good mood. He had his morning buzz. He and Barbara were talking about past shoots and laughing.

I was shocked when I found out the food stylist made $1,200 a day to make food look good. How hard could it be orchestrating parsnips? But it turned out she was a real magician. Apparently actual food does not look appetizing on film. So, she simulated. For us she shaped a substance that was ice cream-like into these perfect round balls with scoop ridges on the bottoms. She made about 20 scoops and placed them on the kitchen table as Johnny looked on.

At that moment Tom Lang, the character actor, came out of the dressing room, looking nothing like Henry the Eighth. If he suggested any of the Tudors, it was Queen Elizabeth.

Johnny suddenly became serious. In fact, he was pissed off.

"When was that headshot of you in the catalogue taken?"

Tom said, "A few years ago."

"Where's your beard?"

"I shaved it off a year ago. I had an impetigo flare up."

"And you are about 50 pounds lighter than in your photo."

"Look man, I was sick. OK? I also had hepatitis. I lost some weight." Johnny looked at me.

"Sam, take his coat and the rest—we got an artificial beard around here somewhere. Take a pillow and stuff it under your shirt for a belly. You're going to be our Henry."

I glanced at Tom. He was clearly about to blow.

"You're going to pay me in full," he said to Johnny.

"I'll talk to your agency," Johnny said.

"If you don't pay me in full, I'm going to sue the shit out of you," he said, and, shaking his head in the direction of Anya, he yelled, "This is bull-shit." He ripped off his costume, stomped to the dressing room to reclaim his street clothes, and made a noisy exit.

I hate conflict of any sort but I have to say my admiration for Johnny was growing. This was a team I wanted to be on.

Anya and I retreated to the dressing room to transform me into Henry the Eighth.

"That was unpleasant," I said to her.

"If you intend a life in commercial photography, get used to it," she replied.

The shoot lasted about an hour and seemed to go well. No mishaps on the set. Everyone was clicking. Johnny announced, "It's a wrap!"

He looked at me. "Good shoot! Now go drop off the film at the lab. When you come back, we'll clean up."

"Sounds good," I said.

Stepping out into the bright early spring sunlight, I had an incredible feeling of satisfaction. We were like a commando unit. We had our mission and we did what we had to do to accomplish it. For the first time in my life, I thought: *This is where I want to be and this is what I want to do.* I ran across Park Avenue South and headed west to the sunny side of the street. I walked through the park toward the Flatiron Building. It was still early so the park crowded with people eating their lunch. There were a few down and out looking people asking for change. I arrogantly gave them my patented, "As soon as I get a job."

I was making it in New York City. I wondered what would have happened if my father had landed in NYC after the war instead of Cleveland. Would he have made it? I supposed he would have lived in Brooklyn where the Jews were. My father, outside of the High Holy days, was not very religious. But how could you believe in a higher power after Dachau?

A cab driver blared his horn at me. I looked up and saw I was standing in the middle of the street. A putz from Ohio. I gestured an apology and stepped back onto the sidewalk. I had passed the lab by half a block.

"Hello, Mr. Sam," Baboo greeted me as I entered. "What do you have for us?"

He, like most of the lab techs in New York City, was from India. I had heard it was all because of a guy named Baldev Duggal. Duggal had opened his own film lab where fellow Indian techs would work and then go off on their own. He had incited a cottage industry. It seemed a new Indian lab was popping up every couple weeks within a four-block radius of Duggal's ground zero.

"Hi, Baboo. We just finished a test shoot of King Henry and his Ice Cream and Johnny would like you to run a clip test on rolls 1a and 1b plus ¼ and deliver ASAP."

I handed him the two rolls of 120mm film and a bag containing another ten rolls. "Hold the ten rolls till you hear from us."

"Very good, Mr. Sam. We will do that. Is this a rush?"

"Absolutely. How long till we see the clips?" I asked.

Baboo replied, with a very welcoming smile, owing to the fact that a rush job doubled his fee, "One and a half hours to your studio."

"Perfect," I said.

I headed back to the studio, walking north along Park Avenue South. I noticed a sudden absence of sunlight, as the sun was eclipsed by the Flatiron Building. Madison Square Park was also in its shadow. I hurried my pace and looked straight ahead. I reached the studio, entered into the dark marble lobby and pushed the elevator button. The door opened and Ong and Johnny's friend Richard Long were arm and arm. When they saw me, they stiffened up.

"Johnny is waiting for you. Tell him I will be back later tonight," Ong said in her thick Thai accent.

"OK," I responded.

In the elevator I pushed number 3. What had I just witnessed? I rode the elevator to the third floor. Stepping out, I hesitated. Johnny and Jennifer were in a serious conversation.

"I thought you said I have a good chance of getting the Arby's account?" Johnny was saying.

"You do, it's just that this art director is being an asshole. He said if I slept with him, you would definitely have the account and I said no! So, he said he would have to consider other photographers. Johnny, I am not going to sleep with him! He's sleezy, plus I'm seeing someone right now." Jenny was tearing up.

"I don't want you to sleep with anyone to get the account, but maybe you can step up the ladder and meet with the art buyer."

Jennifer suddenly smiled. "Actually, that's great idea. I know the art buyer and she will not hit on me."

At that moment they noticed me.

"Don't mind me. I'm just passing through," I said and shrugged my shoulders.

My comment seemed to lighten the moment and Jenny looked back at Johnny and said, "OK I will look into that and talk to you in the morning. Let me know when you get some prints I can take over to the agency." Jenny disappeared into the elevator.

"Well, that was awkward," Johnny said.

"What was?" I said.

"Oh. Nothing, I guess," said Johnny. "Did you see Ong?"

"Ah, I, ah, I saw her coming out the elevator as I was getting in. Why?"

"Just wondering. Was she with anyone?"

I was reluctant to respond but I knew I had to tell him the truth.

"She was with Richard. She said she would see you later tonight."

"OK. So, when is the film clip going to arrive?" Johnny asked, looking pissed.

I rushed the film clips so it should be here within the hour."

"I think it went OK today and you handled yourself really well. You did what you had to do," he said.

"Thanks. I appreciate that," I responded with a big smile.

"As a reward, you want to go up to the apartment and smoke a spliff?"

Now I wasn't much of a weed smoker but I felt this was sort of an initiation into the tribe, so I accepted.

We went up to his apartment.

Besides a few lit Tiffany lamps on a side table, it was dark. The layout was similar to Johnny's studio, but that is where the similarity ended. His apartment was decorated in '60's hippie style. Turkish tapestries and Peter Max and Andy Warhol posters covered the walls. Oversized beanbag chairs and mauve-colored stuffed cushions were randomly strewn around. There were no doors, just hanging walls of colorful beads separating the rooms. I thought that all the place lacked was a soundtrack of the Doors, Hendrix or Joplin. Almost on cue, Johnny started lighting incense. Then he pulled out a bag of weed and rolling papers and proceeded to roll one of the biggest spliffs I had ever seen. He motioned to me to settle in a giant beanbag chair. "Now all we need is little music," he said.

He got up and pulled out an album from one of the milk crates that were housing his massive collection of vinyl.

"You ever see the movie *The Rockers*?" he asked. "Amazing soundtrack, depressing film but, still, sort of uplifting."

"Never heard of it," I replied.

"Check this out."

Johnny dropped the needle of his record player on the track "Money Worries" by The Maytones. As soon as the Reggae started playing, he walked back to the table, picked up the joint and lit it up. He inhaled, and a large plume of smoke billowed into the air.

"Ya Mon, now that is the right stuff," he said as he gyrated to the syncopated beat of the words "Money Worries, Money Worries." He danced toward me and handed me the joint. I took a drag and started coughing immediately. A lightweight. We repeated the ritual a few times and I started to feel myself getting high. Really high. Disoriented, I watched Johnny gyrate around the room, taking deeper tokes.

It was a strange but pleasurable experience: My white Rastafarian boss grooving to the music, pumping his arms in the air.

After some time, Johnny collapsed into the beanbag next to mine.

"So, what did you think of Ong?" he asked.

The question startled me out of my bliss.

"She seems nice," I said diplomatically.

"She's a bitch! And she's sleeping with Richard and it depresses the hell out of me," he said, staring right into my eyes.

"Why don't you tell her to leave?" I offered lamely.

"Because I love her!" he declared.

"Why don't you tell Richard to stay away?"

"He's a good friend. I'm not sure I can do that," Johnny said.

"Well, then I don't know what to tell you," I said.

A long silence followed, broken, finally, by Johnny.

"It's all cool. I'm OK."

We sat back in our beanbag bliss and listened to the album. The buzzer rang. Johnny went to the intercom. It was the studio. Baboo had just delivered the film.

Johnny looked at me.

"Let's go check out King Henry."

In the studio, Johnny grabbed the reel and loaded it. I held my breath and watched him watch the film. Eventually he looked up at me with his reddened eyes.

"This is going to be GREAT!!! You might have a future here," he said. He then told me, "Call the lab and tell them to run rolls A plus ¼, rolls B and C plus one-half and rush it."

"You got it boss," I responded with relief. No, with happiness. I really wanted to be accepted by Johnny.

He asked me, "You hungry? I am. Let's go find some dinner while we wait for the film."

We headed out onto Park Avenue South in the dusk and turned East onto 27th Street, heading toward Third Avenue. It was a muggy evening. The streets were packed with hungry New Yorkers.

Johnny led us to a cafeteria-style Indian restaurant: Gandhi's Gourmet. He instructed me to take a metal plate and fill it up with Dal Bhat, Chana Dal, Alu Gobi, Beef Vindaloo, and Chapati right out the oven.

It was all Greek to me but the smells carried me back to my first encounter with an Indian family. They had just moved in across the street and my Mom asked me to be the neighborhood greeter and bring over some gefilte fish and horseradish to welcome them. Clearly leftovers from Passover. Even at the age of 12 I thought it was odd. I crossed the street and reluctantly climbed the steps to their porch and rang the doorbell. A small Indian woman answered the door wearing a sari. She had a red dot on her forehead.

"Yes, can I help you?" she asked bobbing her head as a sort of greeting.

"Ah, my mom wanted you to have this as a welcome to the neighborhood."

I extended my hands and offered the jar of white fish in water and the jar of red horseradish. She looked at them suspiciously.

"What is it?" she asked.

I explained what was in the two jars and how Jewish people ate this stuff on the holidays and warned her to watch out for the horseradish because it was really spicy. She clearly had no idea what I was talking about, but she smiled nonetheless and took the two jars. I peeked into her house. It was very dark with lots of Persian-looking rugs on the floor and colorful tapestries draping the walls. She thanked me and shut the door.

I was remembering her while Johnny helped me navigate around my plate, warning me what was really spicy and how to use Chapati bread to cool my mouth down. I liked it all. Years of smearing my grandmother's spicy horseradish on gefilte fish had prepared me for this. After we finished Johnny announced we should get back to the studio.

We arrived just as Baboo was delivering the film. He looked at me and smiled.

"What?" I said.

"You're Henry the Eighth, aren't you?" he asked.

"I am, I am," I intoned in my best Herman's Hermits Cockney, although the archaic British Invasion reference was lost on Baboo.

Johnny invited Baboo in for a smoke but he begged off, saying he had too much work still to do.

So, Johnny and I went up to the studio alone and looked at the film.

"What do you think?" I asked when it was over.

"Sam, if we get the Burger King account … it will be because of you. Tomorrow I will make some large color prints and give them to Jenny to take to the art buyer. Hey, do you want a toke before you go?"

"No thanks, I'm good. I guess I'll see you Monday at 8:30?"

"I guess you will, Sam. Enjoy your weekend."

I got into the elevator, rode it down to the street and stepped out into the New York night.

CHAPTER 8

A CHANGE IN THE WEATHER

Paranoia crept into my mind when I walked New York's streets at night. I kept a watchful eye out for anything suspicious and incessantly prepared and revised escape routes in the event of trouble. I never felt alone, though. I didn't have any extended relations or friends or even friends of friends to rely on but I had my invisible protector. I had Luck. It had kept my father alive in the concentration camps and I was his only son. Surely, he had passed it on to me.

When I asked my mom, "What was Dad like before the war?" She would tell me the story of how he left home at the age of 14 to sell rugs across Poland, Germany, Austria, and Switzerland. "That's why he speaks so many languages," she explained. "He would go skiing with his friends in the Alps for days." And she added at the end of every recollection, with a dimpled smile, "He lost his virginity to a prostitute at the age of 14!" knowing this would embarrass me and confuse my adolescent mind.

The man I knew had lost that spark of adventure. He was always looking over his shoulder in public spaces and at night I would hear him wander downstairs to make sure the front door was locked. It was hard to imagine how fearless he must have been as a young man, and lucky. I felt certain he passed on his luck to me, and also his watchful eye.

Arriving home from my first week on the job, I found Howie sitting at our small breakfast–lunch–dinner table, hunched over white powdered lines. "How was your day at work?" he said nonchalantly.

"Great," I said. "What's on the table?"

"Oh, I was walking through Needle Park and this guy came up to me asking if I wanted to score some pure coke. I said no but he kept following me and lowering his prices until it was too good to pass up. So, I ended up buying a gram for 20 bucks. He was desperate, I guess. He looked like a junkie who needed a fix."

"Wait. You bought a gram of coke from a stranger in Needle Park? Are you crazy?"

"Don't talk to me like I'm an idiot. I know my stuff. Plus, for only 20 bucks, what's there to lose? Do you want to try a line or not!"

"I'll pass. It's been a long day and I just want to chill," I said.

He proceeded to place a short straw in his nose and inhaled a line. He looked up at me with a frown. "OK, it's not pure but it does have some kick. It's not burning my nose." He took another snort with his other nostril and suddenly started blowing air out of both nostrils. "This is mixed with something."

He took his forefinger, licked it, and placed it in the bag of white powder. He then withdrew his finger and brushed it on his tongue.

"This shit tastes like baking soda!" he said in disgust.

"So, you bought a $20 bag of baking soda? From a stranger? In Needle Park? We can always put it in the fridge to absorb some of those bad odors." I said.

"There goes my perfect evening," he groused. "I'm going out to get some air." And he left the apartment.

Howie was book smart and street dumb. I felt a little sorry for him due to his awkward appearance. He seemed uncomfortable in his own skin. It didn't help that his last name was Shmeckler, a Yiddish word which, according to my dad, meant "little penis."

I was relieved to be suddenly alone. I was still jazzed about the day and needed some quiet time to process it all. I might have just begun a career as a commercial photographer in New York City.

The next morning the early sunlight woke me. I sat up and looked out the window at the high-rises south of my apartment. Stepping into the living room I found my roommate asleep on the couch, snoring. I decided to go for a jog in Central Park.

I slipped on my sweats and the Harvard T-shirt I bought at Canal Jeans—in the hopes of impressing some girl—laced up my white Converse basketball sneakers and headed out the door. At the elevator, I ran into Cindy.

"Aren't you looking studly!" she kidded me.

"Going for a run to shake off some of this belly fat." I offered lamely.

"I didn't know you went to Harvard," Cindy said.

"Um, well, the T-shirt may have been there, but as for me? Not really. At least not technically. In the academic sense." This made her laugh. I felt encouraged. "Aren't you up awfully early, I mean … for you?" I said, trying with my tone and eyes to establish a connection.

"Tell me about it," she said, again laughing. "I have an early commercial audition for a toothpaste ad." She gave me an exaggerated smile. "What do you think? Do I have the perfect smile or what? My daddy paid a lot for these teeth, and wouldn't it be a hoot if they were pasted to a billboard on the New Jersey turnpike!"

At that moment the elevator opened. We stepped in and stared at the Eduard Munch walls. An awkward silence descended. This was my chance, I thought, to ask her out. She was cute, Jewish, her daddy was rich, and she lived on the same floor. But what if she said no? How awful it would be afterwards to run into her in the hallway! I wouldn't be able to leave my apartment! The elevator opened and Cindy exited, giving an excellent view of her tight-fitting jeans. Now was the time to ask her.

She turned to me. "Have a nice run, Sam."

All I could muster in return was the limp, "Good luck at the audition."

With an all too familiar feeling of self-loathing I darted out the front door and started jogging east toward the park. It was early enough that there were not too many pedestrians. I loved looking at the old buildings as I ran past the ornate architecture and the small retailers on the ground floor. I jogged down 72nd Street and past the famous Dakota Apartments, hoping to catch a glimpse of John Lennon, Lauren Bacall or Leonard Bernstein. I rather doubted though that any of them were awake at this hour. I entered the park, and its green fields and trees and open spaces worked their magic. An hour later I was back in my apartment, feeling rejuvenated. I showered and dressed and headed off to work.

I got to the studio at 8 and no one was there. I turned on the lights and found total disarray. Immediately I went to the safe to see if anything had been stolen. No. It was locked. I walked around looking for clues as to what had happened. The kitchen was a mess, dishes piled high, food on the counter. There were mirrors on the table with traces of white powder. Clearly a debauch! As the dutiful assistant I commenced cleaning. Two hours passed and I was still alone. I wondered if I should head upstairs and to see if Johnny was alright. But just then the elevator door opened and in walked Johnny Strand the Photo Man.

"Hey Sam. When did you get here? Wow, did you clean up the place?"

"Yep," I said. "Looks like you had a little party."

"It sort of started on Friday night after you left and ended sometime this morning.

I think. I'm hungry. Should we order breakfast from Spiro's?"

"Sounds good," I said. "What's on the agenda today?"

Before answering me, Johnny went through an odd routine of closing and opening his left eye, closing and opening his right eye, and finally closing and opening both eyes simultaneously. I assumed he was working out a double vision issue.

"Well, Sam, you did most of the work on Friday. I printed up some shots on Saturday and gave them to Jennifer. She was at the party with her boyfriend. She liked them and now we wait."

Johnny sat down and put his head on the table.

"Ok," I said. "I still have some cleaning up to do. You rest. You look like you need it. By the way, what was the party for?"

"Ong landed a big job with Avedon—which got things rolling. Then her friend Richard came by with some blow and next thing I know a bunch of other people came by to celebrate. The weird thing is Ong and Richard left at some point and I haven't seen them since."

"That is weird," I said, trying to keep my expression neutral. "I hope they're OK."

"Bitch!" Johnny whispered into the table.

The days that followed proved to be as slow as the prior days had been hopping. I decided to organize all the filters, clean all the film holders and paint the floor. As the week progressed Johnny was more and more depressed. He would go upstairs, get stoned, come back to the studio and call Jennifer to lament how his career was ending.

This was exactly what I didn't want to hear. My career couldn't start if his career was over.

It didn't help that Ong would come by with Richard, riding high about the Avedon gig. By the end of the week, Johnny was complaining that money was running out and he would have to cut back. *Great*, I thought, *exactly one week after I thought I made it; I'm going to get fired.*

Just then Jennifer came by. "That art buyer at DDB&O that I was telling you about … they loved the Henry the Eighth photos—loved them—and they want to base the next Burger King ad campaign on the concept. They were going to use Carl Fischer but said you were a better fit! What do you think about that!"

Johnny jumped out his chair and ran up to Jennifer, lifting her and spinning her around. "This is great! This is great! This is great! When do we start?"

"As soon as we draw up the contract. The art buyer said this will be a test campaign and will appear in the Tri-State area first. If it goes well, it could go national."

Johnny turned to me. "Well, it looks like I won't be laying you off, Sam."

Johnny got the Burger King account and started getting other accounts too. The word was out that Johnny Strand the Photo Man was the hot flavor of the month. He also picked up the Progresso Soup and Timex advertising campaign. The studio was buzzing with work.

One afternoon Johnny's father came by to tell him about a new cable show called MTV. "Some music video channel for ze yuut market," his father explained, in an accent I knew well. He introduced himself to me as Kirk Carlawitzski—a name I also knew. He was famous for illustrating the CBS Eye. He was a small, soft-spoken man with round, thick tortoise shell glasses. He looked at Johnny seriously and said, "My boss zinks MTV might be ze next big zing on cable and vants you take portraits of musicians to pitch ze campaign. Do you have time?"

"I can find time," Johnny replied.

Then Kirk turned to me and asked, "How you holding up Sam? Ist Johnny vorking you too hard?"

"No, Mr. Carlawitzski," I said. "I couldn't be happier."

"Vell, you can always come and vork for me if Johnny overvorks you," Kirk said.

"Dad! You work 14 hours a day, 7 days a week! Mom is getting worried about you." Johnny said.

"Your mom always vorried about me, even vhen ve vere in ze concentration camps, but God had other plans for me," Kirk glanced my way.

I said to Johnny, "You never told me your parents were in the camps."

Mr. Carlawitzski answered, "Ve don't talk about it much." Turning to his son he added, "I vill tell my boss you are interested in doing the test shot for MTV." He exited the studio via the stairs.

"Your dad is pretty spry for someone his age and with his history." I said to Johnny.

"Yeah, I don't know how he does it. Let's get busy. We have a lot to set up for tomorrow's shoot."

I wanted to ask Johnny about his father, but I didn't.

The studio was humming for the next couple of months. We were either casting models, discussing the next project or preparing for the next shoot. There was a general euphoria. Ong had started hanging out more, telling us stories about her work with Avedon. Richard was nowhere to be seen.

But then, after two months of continuous work, the phone stopped ringing. Johnny started complaining to Jennifer about the lack of work and disappearing from the studio. Richard was back in the picture and he and Ong would take off in the middle of the day. And I resumed worrying about losing my job. I concluded that this was a schizophrenic line of work.

One day I was in the darkroom mixing chemicals when the phone rang. I was going to let the answering machine take the call when I heard the voice on the other end.

"Johnny, if you are there pick up. I need to speak to Sam. It's URGENT!"

The voice was Mark's. I ran to the phone.

"Mark, it's Sam. Is everything alright?"

"Hey Sam, I've been trying to reach you for the last couple of days. It seems your answering machine isn't on and no one was returning my calls from the studio."

"What's up, Mark? You sound awful!"

"Sam, it's been a while, but I need a big favor from you. I'm in New Mexico and assisting on this major shoot. Originally, we were only going to be here a couple of days but it's been over a week. Now I've been told we have to stay at least another week. I have to get back to New York. My wife just had a baby and…"

"You're a DAD?" I broke in.

"Yeah. I'll fill you in later. The thing is, right now I really need you to come out here and fill in for me so I can get back home. The magazine will take care of all your expenses and you get $500 a week. Can you help me out, bro? I'm really desperate."

"Well, I would like to help you but I think I need to run this by Johnny. Candidly, it is slow here and I could use a change of scenery. Let me ask him when he gets back this afternoon. Tell me more about the gig. Who are you working with and what magazine?"

"It's Isadora Teivel," he said.

"So, you pulled it off! You got the gig!" I said, genuinely happy for him.

"Yeah, I got the gig," Mark said, sounding distinctly less than enthusiastic about his good fortune. "Her former assistant almost OD'd on drugs and she needed someone pronto. And I was there. But look, I got to get going. Let me know ASAP if you can help me out."

"Wait, Mark. How do I get a hold of you?"

"Oh right! We're at the Eldorado Hotel. Just call the desk and ask for Mark O'Reilly."

"One last question, Mark. What's she like to work with?" I asked.

"I got to run Sammy. I hope you can do this for me bro." Mark hung up the phone.

I sat and held the receiver to my ear until the dial tone snapped me out of my revelry. Isadora Teivel, Isadora Teivel, Isadora Teivel. The name was swimming in my mind. She was arguably the top celebrity photographer in the world. I first became aware of "Izzy" when I was 16. I was at a bookstore perusing the photography section when I came across the book, *Young Masters of Contemporary Photography, Teivel and Park*. On the cover were two photos, one of Mick Jagger and the other of a very young Woody Allen. I remember leafing through each page and thinking how cool it would be to meet these people. Now I had the opportunity to assist her. I was numb. Johnny would never let me go. Or would he? I had to at least ask. I began organizing filters and cleaning the 4 x 5-inch film holders. I started cleaning the refrigerator to try to clear my mind. I was beginning to wonder if Johnny would ever show up. Finally, just when I was ready to go, I heard the elevator open.

"Johnny, where have you been? I was just getting ready to leave," I said.

"Hey Sammy. I've been up at my dad's agency trying to drum up some business and then I decided to take a walk. I ran into some old friends and we were just hanging out."

I could tell he'd been smoking weed.

Then he turned all serious on me.

"Sam let's sit down. I have something to discuss with you."

I could tell it was not good news. I decided to hit him with my news first.

"Johnny, I got a call from Mark today and he wants me to assist Isadora Teivel in New Mexico for week so he can come home for a short stint and be with his wife and new baby."

Johnny looked at me in disbelief.

"Mark works for Izzy?"

"Yeah," I said and blabbered on. "Isn't that great! But he told me he was only supposed to be on the New Mexico shoot for a couple of days and it's been a week. He really needs to get back to NYC to see his wife and baby."

"Mark has a baby?" Johnny said, looking confused.

"Yes, a baby. So, he needs me to fly out there ASAP to take over so he can come home. All my expenses will be paid and I will get weekly salary, so obviously you wouldn't have to pay me. It might go for two weeks, I don't know. What do you think?" I asked anxiously.

Johnny looked at me and adjusted his round wire rim glasses. Caressing his beard he replied, "That would be great! For you and for me. With no work coming in and with Ong's spending habits, I was going to have to cut back your hours till something came in. It's only temporary, but this works out even better. So, when do you leave?"

"I need to call Mark back to give him the OK," I said.

"Call him back now, before he changes his mind. Not to scare you but I hear Izzy is really tough to work with," Johnny said. "Like impossible. And she's crazy. And not in the metaphoric sense."

CHAPTER 9

COMMITTING FELONY

I called Mark and got the details. I was to call the magazine with all my info, and they would arrange my flight. Mark would meet me at the Eldorado and "hand me off" to Izzy and then he would fly back to New York. There was one caveat though that Mark threw in: Before I left on the morning flight, I was to pick up a bag of cocaine to bring with me to New Mexico.

I said nothing in response to this and Mark sensed my hesitation.

"Look," he said. "It's really easy. There's a place that Izzy gets her junk from in the Village. You go there, you pick it up, you put the bag in your sock and you get on the plane. No one will ever suspect."

Mark gave me the address of the place and told me to ask for "Queenie." I decided to do the pickup before going home to pack.

I said goodbye to Johnny and told him I would keep him posted as to when I would be coming back. Out in the frigid February air I thought about New Mexico and decided to walk to the West Village to calm my thoughts. I still couldn't believe I was heading out to Santa Fe to assist Isadora Teivel. I also couldn't believe I was going to transport an illegal drug across state lines. A felony offense.

I meandered through the narrow streets of the West Village and came to a gated private road with the vintage sign reading "Waverly Commons." I rang the bell.

"What do you want!" said a scratchy voice through an intercom.

"I'm here to see Queenie."

After a short silence, the gate buzzed, and I pushed my way into an alleyway of narrow townhouses. It was a quiet street and I looked for 18 Waverly. As I approached, I could hear crowd noises. I pressed the buzzer and the same voice spoke to me again.

"Who are you here to see?"

"Queenie. I was sent by Izzy."

The door buzzed and I entered the vestibule. I could not believe the scene. The townhouse was packed to the gills with hip-looking people. It felt like I had just stepped into the party scene from Breakfast at Tiffany's. I soon learned that the party was for an English punk group, the Fabulous Poodles, who were performing at CBGB's. I snaked my way through the crowd and asked where I could find Queenie. My question was met by blank stares until a tall black man with an enormous Afro, wearing an orange Dashiki Caftan shirt, approached me and asked, not unthreateningly, "Why are you looking for Queenie?"

I nervously answered, "Izzy sent me."

He now smiled and put his hand on my shoulder.

"Ah, you're Izzy's new courier boy. She has sent you for her happy dust. Follow me."

We walked down a narrow hallway to a room in the back. He knocked on the door and said, "You have a visitor from Izzy. Can he enter?"

Behind the door I heard a voice say, "He may enter … ALONE."

He looked me in the eye, "You can enter. I will be waiting for you outside this door."

The room was dimly lit. The furniture was covered in red and purple velour fabrics. The ceiling appeared to be a silk parachute. In the center was a large round velvet tufted king-size bed. Lounging in the center was a very corpulent person wearing a plush purple nightgown with voluminous platinum blond hair. "Queenie," I imagined. I wasn't sure if I was looking at a man in drag or an extremely over made-up woman.

"So, Izzy sent you. I haven't seen her in ages. Where has she been?" The voice was raspy.

"I'm not sure. I just started working with her. Well, not actually. I'm about to start working with her. I'm supposed to pick up a special package to take to her in New Mexico." I was stuttering.

"New Mexico! What in the hell is Izzy doing in New Mexico? That girl does get around."

"She's on an assignment for a magazine photographing some actress," I said, trying to sound like I really did work for her.

"Well, it's been a while. I need to remind myself what Izzy likes. Honey, bring that suitcase over to me, the one next to the stuffed leopard."

I looked around the room and saw the leopard. Next to it was a black attaché case. I picked it up and brought it to Queenie, who was now sitting up in the bed. "Mmm," Queenie purred, "You're kind of cute up close."

She stroked my hand when I handed her the case.

"Izzy knows how to pick them. What happened to that last one: Mike? Marty?"

"Mark," I said.

"That sounds about right. The one who looked like John Oats. What did she do to him?"

"Oh, he's still with her. I'm just temporarily helping him out."

She smiled at this.

"Her manikins don't typically last long. In fact, not a one of them lasts long. She squeezes the life out of them. You must be the loyal type, to risk prison and all to bring this to her."

Queenie redirected her gaze to what was inside the attaché case: lots of different sized bags with white powder in them. She felt around the case, picking up different bags, apparently trying to remember which one Izzy liked. "Ah-ha! This is the one. A gram, right? Is that all she wants?"

"I think so," I said, as Queenie handed me the bag.

"Tell Izzy it's time she clears her tab. This is the last one until she does. Will you remember to tell her?"

"I will be sure to tell her. It was a pleasure meeting you."

I turned around to open the door.

Queenie stopped me. "Why are you in such a hurry? Maybe you could stay a while and try some of my goodies." She was fondling her breast. I think.

"Another time," I said. "I have a plane to catch."

I opened the door, and my escort led me through the crowd and out into the cold night.

What the hell was I getting myself into?

CHAPTER 10

IZZY

A limo picked me up at six in the morning at the curb outside my apartment building. The driver introduced himself as Tony and said he took care of Ms. Teivel's people. He handed me an envelope that contained instructions and travel money. Your mission, should you choose to accept it...

I had never been in a limousine before but when my body sank into the soft tan-colored leather upholstery, I was willing to give it a try. There was a bar, a button to call the driver, knobs to set the temperature and magazines in a pouch. I pushed the button that said "Driver."

"Tony, how long before we get to JFK?"

"About an hour and fifteen minutes," he replied.

The *Mission Impossible* theme was running through my brain as I opened the envelope and saw my tickets and itinerary. I would be flying Pan Am to Albuquerque, with a stop in Chicago. I counted the money. Ten crisp $20 dollar bills.

I checked out the magazines. One was the latest issue of *Vinyl Vision* with a portrait of the lead singer of Queen, Freddy Mercury, on the cover. He was shirtless, wearing black leather pants and grinning through a thick black mustache. The headline: "We are the Champions: Freddy's Rise to Fame." I opened the magazine to check the photo credit. Isadora Teivel. I leafed through the magazine, fantasizing what it was going to be like to work with the great Izzy. I must have been lost in this exercise for quite some time because the next thing I noticed was the airport looming in the distance. I had a sudden attack of paranoia: I was about to commit a felony. I pulled up my sock as high as it would go.

After checking my bag at the Pan Am counter, I headed for my gate. Several times I passed uniformed cops but they were uninterested in me. At the security checkpoint a young man looked at my ticket and ran a metal detector up and down my body. My heart was in my throat. He nodded and pointed me to my gate. Nobody gave a damn about the coke! I was on my way to fame and fortune.

In Albuquerque, at the baggage claim, I heard my name called. "Sam, Sam."

I turned and saw Mark walking toward me. We gave each other a hug.

"I wasn't sure you would really come," he said.

"I told you I would. How's your wife and kid?"

"She is totally psyched that I'll be home today. She's climbing the walls with the new baby."

"Well, I'm glad I could help. So, where is Izzy?" I said looking around.

"She's back at the hotel in Santa Fe, still asleep I'm sure," Mark said.

"What's she like?" I asked.

Mark sucked in his cheeks before he answered.

"Oh, she can be difficult. But if you disregard her off-hand comments and just focus on the work, you'll be OK. As far as what your job is, well, you'll set up the lights, load the film, keep the receipts, and make sure she gets up in the morning. Other than that, you'll figure it out."

Mark placed his hand on my shoulder.

"I really owe you Sam. When you get back to New York, I'll take you out for a beer or something even stronger. Here's the car rental contract and keys. You've got a red mustang. It's in the drop-off zone. This is an info sheet with phone numbers and places you'll need to be aware of."

I looked at the piece of paper. It had the hotel address, directions to get there, Izzy's room number and the magazine editor's phone number. At the bottom was written, "Best of luck buddy!" I looked at Mark.

"Um, I have a special package for Izzy. When do I give it to her?"

"As soon as you see her. It will make her very happy and put you on her good side. OK. I got to go. Give my best to Izzy. She knows all about you. I may have exaggerated a bit about your experience, so just improvise."

Mark turned around and walked away.

Improvise? What the hell does that mean?

I stepped out into the bright sunshine and breathed in the dry desert air. It felt great. I located the drop-off zone and saw a red Ford T-top Mustang, a muscle car. It had a ticket on the front window. I threw my bag onto the back seat and grabbed the ticket. $25. I opened the glove compartment and found four more traffic tickets. For speeding.

I headed out of the airport and got onto I-25 North to Santa Fe. I had never been to the Southwest and seeing all the cacti, Juniper and Palo Verde was surreal. I remembered in college seeing images of cacti by Edward Weston and, as beautiful as they were, I never appreciated how otherworldly they look in their natural habitat. Nor had I ever experienced such vast open space as surrounded me, a deep blue sky with soft billowing clouds. I felt an unaccustomed sense of peace. What if I kept driving and never showed up at the job? Izzy might be put out a little but ultimately, would she care? I was a nobody. I could disappear into the desert, change my name, start a new life.

I saw my exit and turned off. Following Mark's directions, I found the Eldorado Hotel. It was classic pueblo revival style. I pulled up to the front doors and was greeted by a man in a uniform who seemed to be expecting me.

"Welcome Mr. Cohen. How was your flight?" he said. He opened the door and I stepped out, looking at the grand entrance adorned with Southwestern artifacts. "May I take your bag, Sir?"

The man grabbed my bag and told me the car would be taken care of by the valet. He led me into the ornate lobby and to the reception desk, behind which stood a very attractive young Latina woman.

"This is Mr. Cohen. He is with Ms. Teivel. Take good care of him."

Boy I could get used to this. I returned the woman's smile. Her name-plate said "Isabella." I suddenly realized I needed to tip the guy. I reached into my envelope and pulled out a 20-dollar bill and handed it to him.

"Thank you, Mr. Cohen," he said. "If there is anything you need, please let me know."

Isabella handed me my room key and I touched the back of her hand with my finger. Maybe a bit creepy, I thought. I waited for the consequences.

"Room 412," she said, with a smile.

I loved my new life! Then I remembered why I was here.

"Is there some way I can get a message to Ms. Teivel?" I asked.

"Oh yes. We will place a message on her phone. We have not seen her today, but she will see the red-light blinking."

"Thank you," I said, smiling one more time at Isabella and I followed the bellboy up to my room.

It felt awkward having someone carry my bags. I wasn't used to being served. I tipped the bellboy $5 and felt relief when he disappeared.

Then I saw the five large rectangular black cases, the long black stand case, and a silver aluminum Zero-Halliburton case on the bed. On the silver case was a note that read, "Sam, inside this case are the cameras, make sure to charge the Hassi every night! In the fridge are the bricks of 120mm film. Be sure to take out a brick the night before and bring an extra brick to the shoot." Forty rolls of film, I thought, that is a lot of film! "There is also a shoot sheet in the silver case. Each setup is to be marked A, B, C ... so A1, A2, B1, B2 etc. Remember to ignore Izzy's abusive comments. And have fun! MARK."

So much for the peaceful easy desert feeling.

I opened the cases. Each had a number and four of them contained a strobe pack and two strobe heads, cords, light sensors. The fifth case had colored gels, more cords, strobe head reflectors, gaffers' tape and a Leatherman. The long cylindrical case contained light stands, clamps and more extension cables. Next to all the cases was an expandable two-wheeled cart and a duffle bag with more gaffers tape, extension cords and collapsible silver and gold reflectors that we crudely called elephant diaphragms.

I felt panic. In the studio everything was stationary and in its place. It dawned on me that location photography was a studio on wheels. All this stuff needed to be transported! I opened up the silver case which contained two Hasselblad ELX bodies, lenses, a Polaroid back, lens tissues, three Hasselblad backs, a couple of sharpies, a lens shade and assignment sheet forms. The camera case weighed around 40 lbs.

I began to see why Mark was burning out. I sat on the bed and looked at all the stuff I had to schlep and wondered how I was going to manage. I wanted to go down to the bar and have a few drinks but I knew I had to wait for Izzy to call. Lying down on the bed I closed my eyes and fell asleep.

I had a dream. I arrived at a photo shoot totally unprepared. I loaded all the film backs wrong and forgot the light meter. A scary-looking woman with hair like Medusa's started yelling at me: "You are a mistake. Go back to Ohio and work for your dad. You'll never make it as a photographer!" I tried to respond to her, but nothing came out of my mouth. The scary woman threw the camera backs at me. I ducked my head to get out of the way ... and in doing so must have hit my head on the camera case. I woke up.

Sweat was dripping down my face. I looked outside. It was dark. The phone on the bedside stand was flashing. "Oh Shit!" I thought. I had missed her call.

I called the receptionist to retrieve the message.

"Yes, Mr. Cohen. Ms. Teivel called about 10 minutes ago and wants to meet you in the bar at 10:30."

"What time is now?" I asked.

"It is 10:25," the operator said.

"Thank you." I slammed down the phone. I looked in the mirror: I looked awful. I took off my wrinkled shirt and ran my head under cold water and shook out my long curly hair. My hair always seemed to take care of itself when I ran it under water and shook it. In middle school, my friend and the guy who introduced me to photography, Dave Lindsey, called me Water Buffalo. I put on a black T-shirt and a casual lightweight jean jacket. I took one more look in the mirror: still awful.

I took the elevator down to the lobby and walked into the bar. It was dimly lit. Soft mariachi music was playing through the speakers. I looked around and saw, sitting at the bar, a woman wearing a black leather jacket. She was sipping a glass of red wine. She had wild hair like Medusa. I took a deep breath and approached her.

"Ms. Teivel?"

She turned. Her hair was nondescript brown and shoulder length. She wore large tortoise shell glasses that were held in place by a notably large Romanesque nose.

"Are you Sam?" she asked in low raspy voice.

"Sam I am," I said, having no clue why I suddenly decided to turn into Dr. Seuss.

"Okay," she responded, looking at me like I was the jerk I just proved myself to be. Her eyes wandered up and down my body. Then she spoke again.

"Let's establish the rules. First, don't call me Ms. Teivel, I am not your teacher. Call me Izzy. It's easy to remember. Can you remember that?"

"Yes, ma'am," I replied sheepishly. This is not going well.

"And don't call me ma'am either. Just Izzy. Now sit down and order a drink. We need to go over tomorrow. Mark said you paid a visit to Queenie. Did you bring it?"

"It's in my room. Do you want me to get it now?"

"Not right now. You can bring it to my room after we go over the drill for tomorrow."

The bartender came by and asked what I wanted.

"Scotch on the rocks," I said, again not knowing why I said it. I was not a drinker and I had never had Scotch, much less Scotch on the rocks, in my life.

"A Scotch man!" she said, and her eyes once again traveled over my body.

"Given where we are, I suppose I should have ordered a Tequila," I said.

Izzy slid her wine glass away from her.

"Cancel that Scotch," she growled at the waiter. "Bring us two glasses and a bottle of Tequila. Make sure it has the worm."

The bartender brought two shot glasses and a bottle of Tequila with lemon and a small bowl of salt.

Izzy looked at me without a smile. "I guess we'll be here awhile."

I poured the Tequila into both shot glasses and raised my glass. "Here's to a successful shoot." We clicked glasses. She downed hers in one gulp. I imitated her example.

There was a worm in the bottle. She fished it out and handed it to me.

"Eat it," she said.

I hesitated. The thing was disgusting.

Her brown eyes peered into mine through the tortoise glasses.

"I need to know you're ready for anything," she said.

I swallowed the worm.

There followed a strange interlude during which she looked at me and I could think of nothing else to do but look back at her. I felt this was some sort of challenge or test, but to what end I had no idea. It was just very weird. I finally thought of something to say to end it. "You know Izzy, Mark didn't tell me much about the assignment…"

"You know what? I'm glad Mark didn't tell you much about the assignment. Do you know WHY? Because you are now working for me. I will tell you about the assignment. And guess what? You are not to tell anyone else about the assignment. WHY? Because if you do, I will make your life miserable. You got that?"

I nodded as if I were a bobblehead.

"Vinyl thinks I am on vacation, but I am actually on assignment for another magazine. It's a cover shot but won't appear in print for three months. That will give me time to figure out which magazine I want to work for."

"OK," I said, realizing how much I still had to learn about life at the top. "So, like, who are you photographing?" I poured us both another shot and chugged mine.

"Here's a hint. It's a she and she just became famous."

"Does she have a name?" I asked. The Tequila was kicking in.

Izzy looked at me, and slowly, very, very slowly, she emptied her glass before speaking.

"Thelma Zinger. Do you recognize the name?"

"The *Soldier Boy*?" I said.

"For the record, her co-star Mitchell Dear was a total dick to her." Izzy grabbed the bottle and poured herself—but not me—another shot and downed it. "I've been down here a week and only had one session with her, which sucked. I can't get the portrait I want."

I took the bottle and refilled my glass.

"What type of portrait do you want," I asked.

"That's a dumb question. I won't know till I'm there."

I guzzled my shot, Izzy-like, only to instantly regret it. My head was starting to spin.

"OK, then," I said. "What's the schedule tomorrow?" I needed to wrap things up and retreat safely to my room.

"The schedule? The schedule, Sam, is you pack the car, we meet at 2 PM in the lobby, and we head over to where Thelma's staying, about half an hour outside of Santa Fe."

I stood up and immediately felt dizzy. I steadied myself on the stool. Izzy signed the tab and said, "Let's go to your room so I can pick up my present."

When she stood up, I could see she was much shorter than me. She looked up into my eyes. "I have a rule. I don't sleep with my assistants. So don't get the wrong idea when I come to your room."

"Oh, don't worry," I said. I grabbed hold of the counter of the bar to steady the room.

She now dramatically presented herself to me.

"Don't you think I'm attractive?"

I assumed she was being facetious. "How could I not?" I said. I was worried I might hurl at any moment.

She was imposing and very serious. "Your lying!" she said, and her eyes once again wandered up and down my body. "But that's OK. I will let you off the hook. This time."

We went up to my room and I grabbed the bag of cocaine and handed it to her and said, "Before I forget, Queenie said, no more until you pay your tab."

"Fuck that!" Izzy said, turning around and storming out of the room. I ran to the bathroom and started vomiting into the toilet.

CHAPTER 11

THELMA AND IZZY

The next morning, I lay in bed watching the desert sun stream into the room and highlight the Georgia O'Keefe prints hung on sand-textured walls. I was still in my clothes and the silver case was on the bed. I suddenly realized I hadn't charged the cameras. I looked at the clock. 9:30. I checked to see if the red light on the phone was blinking. It wasn't. No messages. I charged up the Hasselblad and decided to spoil myself and order room service. Egg's ranchero, fresh orange juice, a tortilla. I jumped into the shower and started feeling good again. I could get used to this. Sleeping in late. Eating well. And all paid for by someone else. Fifteen minutes later I heard a knock on the door. I put on the oversized terrycloth plush white robe and opened the door. A young Hispanic woman pushed a cart in and laid out my breakfast on a table. "Anything else you need?" she asked. I resisted the impulse to be a jerk, and just said "No." I gave her a five-dollar bill. "Muchas gracias, señor!" she said with a big smile, and she turned around and exited the room.

I had to figure out how to pack everything into the Ford T-Top mustang. I rang for the bellboy. He arrived and piled everything onto a cart and rolled it outside to the car. I told him I'd take it from here and gave him a five-dollar bill. I opened the trunk and started fitting the cases in. After about three tries of loading and unloading I figured out how to make it fit. By the time I finished I felt like I had just run a marathon. The sun was hot and my T-shirt was drenched in sweat. I asked the concierge to watch the car, tipping him with my now standard fiver, and ran up to my room to change. It was almost 2 PM and I expected Izzy to appear at any moment.

I dressed and returned to the cool shade of the entryway, keeping an eye on the car, and waited. 2:15. 2:30. No Izzy. Something must be wrong. I got the concierge to call her room but there was no answer. I gave the concierge another fiver to watch the car and ran to her room. "Izzy! Izzy!" I said, trying to keep calm as I knocked on her door. No answer. Great! She had overdosed and I would be blamed for the bad coke. This is how I'd make it onto page one of the *New York Post*. "Izzy!" "IZZY!" Finally, the door opened and there stood the famous Isadora Teivel, her hair looking like snakes. She was wearing only a long white button-down shirt.

"What the fuck is going on?"

"Izzy, we were supposed to be on the road half an hour ago."

"Then why the fuck didn't you wake me up earlier?"

I opted not to answer this.

"Shit! I'll call Thelma and tell her my fucking rookie assistant fucked up the very first fucking thing he was supposed to fucking do. Wait for me down by the car. You did pack the car, didn't you?"

"It's all packed and ready to go. I'll wait for you in the lobby," I said. She slammed the door.

I waited in the lobby for an hour. When Izzy finally appeared, her hair was wet from the shower and she was wearing blue jeans along with the white button-down shirt, and gray Saucony running shoes.

"Let's go," she said, not looking at me.

The doorman opened the car door for her. I gave him a five-dollar bill and got into the driver's seat. Izzy stared at me. "Did you just give him a five-dollar tip for opening the door?"

"Is there a problem with that?" I asked.

"Only if you consider stupidity a problem! You don't tip someone five dollars for opening a fucking door! You do that again and I will take it out of your wages. I hope you're keeping track, for the expense report, of all the cash you're giving away."

"I am," I said—though I was not—and I started the car. We took off and said not another word.

"Turn right off this ramp and right at the stop sign." Izzy was speaking to me again. I obeyed the instruction. "Now take a right at that stop sign and head up the mountain till you see the first adobe house."

"OK," I said.

I pulled up to a sand-colored home and parked.

Thelma Zinger strolled out of the house, wearing a long cotton skirt and a sleeveless white T-shirt. She had on a pearl necklace and turquois bracelets on both arms. "You made it," she said by way of greeting.

Izzy got out of the car, walked up to her and kissed her on the mouth.

"So sorry about being late. My substitute assistant mixed up the times. How are you darling? Is your day going well?"

"I spent the morning at the spa. Then lunch with my agent. So, I'm glad you're late. I needed the extra time."

Izzy put her arm around Thelma.

"This is Sam. He flew out from NYC to take Mark's place. Mark wasn't feeling well."

I walked up to the famous actress and extended my hand.

"Pleased to meet you, Ms. Zinger. I really enjoyed your last movie," I said.

"Why thank you, Sam," she said. She had a pleasant Midwestern manner.

She turned to Izzy. "What are we going to do today? My agent says I have to fly back to LA for an audition with Spielberg this weekend. I fly out tomorrow evening."

I could tell Izzy was not happy about this news. I suspected she was hoping to stay longer on the client's expense account.

"I thought we would do some interiors of you in your bedroom and kitchen and go from there." She turned to me. "Sam, set up some lights inside and let me know when you have a final Polaroid. Thelma and I will be by the pool."

I pulled the cases out the car and set them in the shade of the porch. I was familiar enough with Izzy's published photos to have an idea of how to set up the lights for her. It took me about 2 hours. I took the Polaroids and brought them to Izzy. She and Thelma were drinking red wine. Izzy looked at the Polaroids carefully.

"Start over. This is over-lit. I want the bedroom to look dark and dreamy and the kitchen to look as if early morning light is pouring through the French doors." She handed me back the Polaroids. "We are short on time so make it quick."

Since all the lights were on the stands, I started over and returned in 45 minutes. This time Izzy approved them. She and Thelma got out of their lounge chairs, stumbling and giggling.

Thelma put her hand on my shoulder and asked me, "Sam, are you a member of the tribe?"

It took me a second to get what she was saying.

"You mean am I Jewish? Is it that obvious?"

"You know, Sam, I grew up in a Hassidic home in Cleveland Heights. I was the only girl out of five kids. I hated it and rebelled and left home when I was 15." She winked at me. "I still have a thing for Jewish boys."

Before I could share that I too was from Cleveland, Izzy had grabbed her arm and pulled her into the house. I followed and was surprised by a German Shepard growling at me, looking ready to attack.

"Frank, NO! Down Boy!" Thelma commanded. She walked up to him and hugged him, stroking his head. "He is really a gentle puppy dog and a luvie wuvie, aren't you Frank? He only looks mean," she said in a baby voice.

"He looks like he could rip a person apart if he wanted to," I said.

"Only if someone tried to harm me," Thelma replied, hugging the dog tighter.

I looked at Izzy, who was stroking her chin and observing Thelma and the dog very intensely, as if she were hatching an idea. She must have sensed I was staring at her because she looked at me and snapped, "We'll start in the kitchen. Darling, I want you to wear that cute yellow apron and a pair of panties and nothing else."

Thelma said, "What a great idea." I thought so too.

Thelma left the room to change, and Izzy turned to me sternly. "I do not want you to talk to her unless she asks you a question! You got that? Are all the camera backs loaded?"

"Yes," I replied.

"Good. We'll do some shots here and then in the bedroom. After you reload the backs for the shoot in the bedroom, your job is done, and you can head back to the hotel."

"But what about the breakdown and packing the lights?" I asked dutifully.

"You can come back in the morning around 9:30. I want to do one more shot outdoors and then you can pack up." Just as Izzy was about to say something else, Thelma Zinger walked out of the bedroom looking like every college boy's fantasy of a maid.

"What do you think?" she said to me. I was about to answer when I looked at Izzy. I said nothing. I just smiled.

Thelma walked up to me and, turning her back, said, "Sam, could you tie the back, so it doesn't fall off?" I looked at Izzy for approval and she nodded. I tied the yellow tie in a bow trying not to touch her skin. I noticed she had a tattoo of the Star of David on her right shoulder blade. Just as I finished tying the bow she bent over, bumping her ass into my crotch, and giggled.

"Sorry Sam, I had a cramp."

I looked at Izzy and shrugged my shoulders. She was clearly not happy with me.

"OK, let's get started," Izzy announced. She directed Thelma in some provocative poses around the kitchen. Bending over the sink washing dishes. Bending over the kitchen table reading a glamour magazine. "Give me sexy." "Be melodramatic." "Good, now let me see jealous." I ran around adjusting the key light and hair lights and reminding Izzy to take a Polaroid with every light change. I reloaded the camera backs. I was feeling useful for the first time since I'd arrived in New Mexico.

I could tell Izzy had no clue about the technical side of photography. The thought occurred to me that maybe I could leverage my knowledge here to balance the work relationship. The day-to-day grind of the year I had worked for Johnny might pay off after all. Izzy seemed to be happy with the lighting adjustments I was making. Then Izzy took a break and told Thelma to bring out the Tequila. A bottle appeared and Thelma set out three shot glasses.

"We only need two glasses, darling," Izzy said.

Thelma looked at me as Izzy said, "Sam has to drive back tonight and should not be drinking."

Deflated again. After they downed a couple of shots, Izzy turned to me and said it was time for a wardrobe change and a change of scenery. I reloaded the three camera backs. Izzy then said to me, "I can take it from here. Leave everything and come back tomorrow."

As I was walking out the door, I overheard Izzy saying to Thelma, "Now for your surprise, darling: A little snow in the desert."

Driving back to the hotel, I couldn't help but feel frustrated. I sensed Thelma wanted to talk to me. And I wanted to ask her about growing up in Cleveland. In a Hassidic home no less! Seeing the Star of David tattooed on her back triggered so many memories. But Izzy shut it all down. She wanted Thelma for herself.

When I got back to the hotel and headed for the bar. I scanned the mostly empty room to see if there were any solo women. Nope. But I did see the cute receptionist at a table chatting with a couple of friends. I decided to sit at the bar and have a drink.

I ordered a beer. The bartender poured a Corona into a pilsner glass and split a quarter lemon on the rim. I nursed the drink, staring at the mirrored wall of beverages in front of me. I looked back to see if the receptionist was still at the table with her friends, but they were gone. I decided to finish my drink and head upstairs. I looked at my watch. Only 9 PM. I could zone out on TV and possibly find some lube.

"Hola, Señor Cohen. Is everything going well with your visit?"

I turned toward the voice. It was Isabella, the receptionist. Solo.

"Where are your friends?" I asked.

"Oh, they have early mornings, so they left. What are you doing all by yourself at the bar?"

"Ah, my boss gave me the night off. I thought I would come down here to unwind. Do you have time for a drink? My treat."

"I am off until tomorrow evening," she said. "You know, why not?" She sat down on the stool next to me.

I asked her what she'd like and she said what I was drinking would be fine. I gestured to the bartender and soon another Corona appeared.

"So, what do you do when you're not greeting the guests?" I asked.

"I am either studying or taking care of my grandmother. Not much else," she said. "Where are your parents?" I asked.

"Back in Mexico, with the rest of the family. I was lucky enough to come here when I was 12 and live with my grandmother. She raised me."

"Well, she has done a fine job!" I said, raising my glass to toast her, thinking how my dad had survived immigration to America with $50 to his name and no English, carrying with him the ghosts of Old Europe.

"What are you studying?" I asked.

"I am studying to be a nurse. As far as I know I am the first in my family to go to college," she said, with obvious pride.

I could not help staring at her full lips. I imagined taking her in my arms. She talked about her harrowing migration story, how her mother insisted she leave home for El Norte, how she paid a "coyote" to take her across the border and her terror at what might happen on the way. Miraculously she made it unharmed to her grandmother's house. She told me how her family struggled back in Mexico, how she sent money to them whenever she could. We were on our second beer when I reached over and put my hand on hers. She looked at me and smiled and put her hand on my thigh. Without saying a word, we walked out of the bar together and headed to my room.

I woke up the next morning feeling a gentle warm breeze blowing across my face. Next to me was a beautiful woman with toffee-colored skin, long black hair and the most sensuous lips I had ever seen. On the side of her neck was a tattoo I hadn't noticed the night before. "AZTECA."

It was already 9 and I had to get going. I kissed Isabella on the cheek and got up to take a shower. Stepping out the shower I saw her sitting up on the bed staring at the window. "Buenos Dias," I said, exhausting all the Spanish I knew.

"Hi," Isabella replied in a distant way.

"Why the sad face?" I asked.

She started crying.

"What's wrong?" I said, and I sat down next to her.

"My boyfriend will not be happy about this," she said.

"Boyfriend?" I said. "First, I didn't know you had a boyfriend. And second, why would he ever find out?"

"People talk and this is a small town. He is in a gang."

"A gang! He's in a gang? Like the kind that carries guns and shoots you if they don't like the way you look, that type of gang?"

"They are not that bad, but he could do some harm if he found out," she said with eerie calm.

"Harm! But he won't find out. Right? How could he find out?"

She looked away. She whispered, "Si Dios quiere."

Oh God! Oh Jesus! Oh Moses. I imagined myself being tied up and dragged by a motorcycle down a dirt road.

"OK. Here's what we do. I will get dressed and leave, and you will wait half an hour—half an hour!—before you leave. You understand?"

She nodded.

"Why didn't you tell me about this last night at the bar?" I said.

"I don't know. I was lonely and the idea of making love to a famous photographer was a turn on."

A famous photographer!

I headed out of the hotel looking around to see if I was being followed. I couldn't help thinking that everyone who worked there knew. I gave the valet my ticket for the car. He stared at me and nodded. He knew! He was probably part of the gang. They were going to follow me into the desert and run me off the road and kidnap me just like in the movie *A Touch of Evil*. No one would ever know. The red T-Bar Mustang pulled up. I tipped the valet $10 in hush money and drove off. *Another Sunny Day in*

Paradise I thought as I drove down the highway, keeping my eye on the rearview mirror.

I arrived at Thelma Zinger's rental house and parked the car. Walking to the front door, I was confronted by the German Shepard in killer mode. "Frank! FRANK! Stop! Stop!" Thelma yelled. She appeared and pulled Frank off the door. She turned around and announced, "Izzy, it's your assistant. What should I tell him?" ("Assistant?" What happened to the "Sam" of yesterday?) She dragged Frank to a back room and I waited.

A few minutes later—like five minutes later—Izzy came to the door, wearing just her white button-down shirt. "Why are you here so early?" she kvetched.

"I'm here right on time, the time you told me to arrive," I replied.

"Well, you can start by taking down the lights in the kitchen and then the bedroom. We are doing one outdoor shot today so set up a light for outside." Izzy disappeared into the bedroom. I went to work.

By the time had I packed up the lights in the kitchen, Izzy and Thelma had come out of the bedroom. In passing I noticed they were wearing matching white button-down shirts and nothing else.

"What are you looking at?" Izzy said.

"Nothing," I said. "Can I go into the bedroom and pack up the lights?"

"You can go into the bedroom and jerk off!" Izzy replied.

"OK," I said, thinking it was impossible that my day could go from really, really bad to worse.

The bedroom was a mess. Sheets were strewn about. Empty liquor bottles littered the floor. On the dresser was a mirror covered with white powder residue. I started packing up the lights wondering if and how I was going to survive this day. I walked into the kitchen and Izzy and Thelma looked up from the kitchen counter.

"Where do you want me to set up the outdoor light?" I asked.

Izzy got up and pointed out the kitchen window. "By the cactus garden out there and you better do it fast while the light is good."

"OK," I said.

Never having set up an outdoor light before, I was a bit nervous, which was good because it took my mind off the possibility of being executed by some gang member when I got back to the hotel. I remembered that Mark had described how to set up the outdoor light. I finished the set up and tested the lighting by taking a polaroid of the stand case. I brought it to Izzy for her approval and braced myself for another acerbic response. I was surprised when Izzy looked up from the polaroid and said, "Nice background. Let's shoot."

We all headed outside to the location, Thelma still wearing her button-down white shirt, panties and flip-flops, with her dog following. "OK, Thelma, I want you to get down on the ground and play with your dog," Izzy commanded. As if under a spell, Thelma complied.

"Are we ready to shoot?" Izzy said to me.

"Ready, whenever you are," I replied, handing Izzy the camera that was synched to the strobe light. That is when I realized Izzy had broken down any defenses or inhibitions Thelma might have had. Whatever Izzy told Thelma to do, she did. A great movie star crawling around the desert, wrestling with her dog as if they were lovers. That was Izzy's genius.

After about 20 minutes of shooting, Izzy announced, "It's a wrap!" Thelma got off the ground, brushed the sand off and walked up to Izzy, "Do you think you got what you needed?"

"I think so. We can call it a day. Anyway, you have a plane to catch. Sam, pack up all the gear while Thelma and I say our goodbyes."

At first, I was relieved that the shoot was finished but, as I started to pack up, I remembered we had to go back to the hotel. The shoot was over, and we were heading back to my doom.

"I want to drive!" Izzy said with a weird smile and she pushed her glasses up onto her nose.

"OK," I replied and gave her the keys. Maybe this was the little bit of luck I needed. Isabella's boyfriend would mistake Izzy for me since she was driving and knock her off. I could imagine the *NY Post* headline. "Dizzy Izzy Dead!"

I was jarred out of my pleasant daydream when I realized Izzy was driving 30 miles over the speed limit.

"This car has guts! Take the wheel Sam and push the pedal to the metal," Izzy shouted.

"It's not safe" I said.

"Do it!" she yelled, and she pulled me over towards her and put my left hand on the steering wheel as she simultaneously pushed her foot further down on the accelerator.

I looked at the speedometer. We were over the 100-mph mark.

"Please slow down, Izzy," I pleaded. "You're going to kill us."

"Put your foot on the gas pedal, Sam, and I will let you take over the accelerator."

"OK, Izzy, OK," I simpered and I put my left foot on top of her right foot. She slipped her foot away from the pedal and my foot took control. She then shimmied her way off the seat and stood up holding onto the T-bar. "Faster, go faster," she screamed.

I was letting up on the pedal. I looked and saw her long hair flying back and forth. She had a large shit-eating grin on her face. She commanded, "Faster, I said!"

I pushed slowly down on the gas pedal and the faster we went the louder Izzy would scream. She was crazed. I entertained the thought of her flipping out of the car and driving on. Then she screamed, "STOP THE CAR! STOP THE CAR, NOW!"

I slowed down and pulled the car over to the side. Looking at Izzy I said, "Now what?"

"My glasses flew off my head and I can't see without them. We have to go back and find them NOW! I don't have another pair and I have to go off to LA after this.

YOU HAVE TO FIND THEM!" She was hysterical.

(I have to find them? Why me? I'm not the maniac who decided to stand up on the car seat while driving 110 mph!)

"OK," I said. "Let's go find them."

It was now dusk. We had about an hour of light. I turned the car around and turned the headlights on and slowly drove down the middle of the road. Fortunately, there were no other vehicles on this remote stretch of desert road. After about 15 minutes of slow driving, I saw a glimmer on the road. I stopped the car and left the headlights on, walking towards the reflection. I could not believe I had actually found her glasses. I picked them up and walked back to the car.

"Well?" said Izzy anxiously.

I held out the glasses and she grabbed them.

"That was a stupid thing to do. You drive back to the hotel," she said.

Why you ungrateful bitch, I thought.

"OK," I said.

We got back to the hotel and the bellboy came out for our bags. Izzy was in business mode.

"Sam, we leave for the airport at 8 AM. I am off to LA. You go back to NYC and hand the film over to Mark. Be sure it's all labeled. Mark will know what to do."

I helped the bellboy load the cases onto the cart and looked around for Isabella or one of her friends. No one in sight. When I walked into the hotel lobby, there was a male receptionist where Isabella had been the day before. I walked up to him and asked him where the young lady was.

"She called in sick today, sir, but she should be back tomorrow evening. Would you like to leave a message for her?"

"No, no," I said. "Forget I even asked." I handed him a five-dollar bill.

CHAPTER 12

BACK TO NYC

The flight to New York City gave me time to process the Santa Fe episode. How did Mark cope with Izzy's neurotic behavior and insane travel schedule? I felt like I had been gone for a month. It was a relief to be heading back to a sane and familiar environment. Johnny's world was what it was: a roller coaster of too much work and then not enough work, while he sedated himself with pot and denied the fact that Ong was sleeping with his friend Richard. OK. Maybe not ideal. But still a better fit for me than Izzy's world. I knew what to expect and his personality suited mine. In any case, I was sure I would never hear back from Izzy. I drifted off to sleep, until a voice announced, "Please extinguish your cigarettes, pull up your seats, and fasten your seatbelts. We will be landing at JFK airport in 20 minutes." I pulled up the window shade and looked out. Below was the stainless steel Unisphere, a miniature remnant from the 1964 World's Fair. I was back to the place I called home.

Walking through the terminal, I clutched the camera case and bag full of film. At the baggage claim I heard my name being called out. Looking up, I saw Tony, dressed in his dark blue driver's uniform with its pressed white shirt, thin black tie and black cap. He was holding up a sign. "Welcome Home Sam."

"How goes it with Ms. Teivel?" Tony asked.

"I guess we will see when the film's developed," I answered.

"Naw," he said. "I'm sure it all went well. Mark had only good stuff to say about you. Speaking of, he's at the studio and you're to hand him the shot film before I take youse home."

Together we collected the seven large black cases from the conveyor belt, loaded them on two carts, and headed out of the terminal toward parking.

Merging onto the BQE, we zoomed by the diverse neighborhoods of Queens.

"Tony, anything exciting happen while I was gone?" I said to break the silence.

"Not much. Some sort of scandal with the mayor's office. The Jets still suck. And the weather is what it is. Did Ms. Teivel behave herself?" he asked.

"Doesn't she always," I laughed.

"I'm sure she does," Tony said. I think we both understood not to gossip about the boss.

We reached her studio on 31st street between 6th and 7th Avenues and Tony got out to open the door for me, "Why don't you buzz her studio and see if Mark can come down and help us?"

"Sure, but what number do I push?"

"Oh, right, you've never been here before. Push 4B and see if you get a response."

I pushed the button, heard a buzz and waited. A scratchy-sounding voice responded. It was Mark.

"Hey Mark, I'm here with all the equipment and film," I said.

"Be right down, bro. Glad you made it back."

I wasn't sure what he really meant by that.

Mark appeared and gave me a hug. "Well, how did it go?" he asked.

"I'll tell you when we get to the studio," I said, nodding my head toward Tony.

We hauled the equipment into the freight elevator and in silence we rode up four floors to Izzy's studio. When the door opened and I could see the studio was deserted, I turned to Mark.

"She is crazy! No, let me rephrase that. She is PSYCHOTIC. How do you put up with her?"

Mark turned defensive.

"Alright, she can be impossible, it's true, but whenever I tell anyone who I work for, they are always impressed. I figure she will be a stepping-stone to a terrific job somewhere. So, I put up with her antics. Plus, she's harmless. For the most part."

I looked around the studio and was surprised to see the walls void of any images.

"Looks kind of empty here," I said to Mark.

He looked around trying to comprehend my comment.

"Oh, you mean the empty walls and no furniture and stuff. Yeah, Izzy doesn't like any distractions when the celebs come by. She likes all the attention on her. Hey, we'll just leave the equipment by the front door, since I fly out tomorrow morning to L.A."

I followed him to the back of the studio, where there was a gray metal desk and two black chairs. We sat down to sort through the film and receipts.

"How's your wife and baby?" I asked.

"Just great! Valerie was really happy to see me. I don't think the baby cared."

He sorted through the receipts. "Wow, you tipped a lot!"

"Was I supposed to write down all the tips?" I asked.

"Sort of. I think it may be a good idea to change the amount of some of the tips to … oh, what the hell, it will drive Sanjeet crazy. Let's keep them."

"Sanjeet?" I asked.

"Her accountant. You'll meet him next week when you hand him your invoice."

"I have to hand him my invoice? Can't I just mail it to him, or leave it with Izzy?"

"Not if you want to get paid this year. If you mail it, Sanjeet will bury it somewhere and Izzy never handles money. It all looks good," Mark said, looking up at me. "I'm going to have Tony take me to the lab and then home. Do you want a lift?"

"No, I need to decompress. I think I'll walk and take the subway home."

"Thanks for doing this for me, Sam. I owe you big time. Val isn't too happy that I'm gone a lot, especially with the new baby and all. I'm not sure how long I can stick it out with Izzy, but I need to stay a little bit longer, until I make some more contacts and get my portfolio together."

"I'm not sure I can fill in for you again, working with Johnny and all. You're right about Izzy, though. If you can get past her abuse, it's a pretty cool gig." I paused and then asked, "Is Izzy gay?"

Mark looked at me. "Depends on who or what she is with at the time."

We both burst out laughing. I said my farewell to Mark as we stood on the street and told him to stay in contact. He got in the limo and Tony closed his door. Tony turned to me, "It was good to meet you Mr. Sam. I hope we meet again."

"You never know, Tony. You take care," I replied, and I watched the black limo drive off. I looked around and took a deep breath and started walking and reflecting on the past four days.

I meandered down Sixth Avenue. By the time I reached Times Square, I wasn't far from home and decided I could walk the rest of the way.

I had never walked around Times Square in the evening and its salacious appearance was fascinating. No wonder the photographer Diane Arbus was drawn to this part of town. All the sex clubs and porno movie houses trying to lure you in with a carnival atmosphere. "Live Sex, Midget Sex, Orgies, Hot Ladies, Glory Holes, Hot Tubs and more," announced a tall thin Black man dressed in tight-fitting white bellbottoms, a white jacket, a black button-down shirt with wide collars and an oversized white fedora. "All for only five bucks. Come on, man. It will be the time of your life!" He raised one hand up in the air and the other hand directed me to the door. I snapped out of my mellow state of mind and picked up my pace, passing by scantily dressed prostitutes and overly dressed pimps trying to lure me into their lairs. I was suddenly feeling very uneasy and had the impulse to run but resisted. That would be uncool and suspicious looking.

I remembered in middle school, walking at night in my neighborhood, I passed two greasers who looked at me as if I were an oddity. I thought I dodged a bullet when I heard, "Isn't that the Kike with curly hair?" On the upbeat, I started running faster than I had run in my life. I heard a gunshot and laughter as I distanced myself from them, not stopping till I reached the front door of my home.

Instinctively, I picked up my pace until I got to 47th Street and things started to quiet down. Still unsettled, I decided to catch a cab home.

"Hi Jesus, who's your friend?" I said entering the lobby.

"Hi, Mr. Sam. This is my son, Carlos. He will be taking my place for a while. I'm going on vacation," Jesus said.

"Hi Carlos, welcome to the club," I said.

"Club?" Carlos replied.

"Never mind, just happy to back," I replied, giving them a wave as I walked to the elevators. The door of the elevator opened and a young couple pushed past me. I stepped in, put my bag down, and pressed 19. The song "Sailing" by Christopher Cross was playing softly in the background. As I entered the apartment, I found Howie on the couch making out with a girl. Startled, she jumped up. "Oh, hi, you must be Howie's roommate," she said, extending her hand.

"That's me. Nice to meet you."

"I'm Sherry, Sherry Finkelstein. Howie's friend from Rosemount," she said nervously.

Howie interjected, jumping from the couch. "Hey, I thought you weren't coming home till tomorrow."

"Nope. Today. Didn't you get my note?" I said.

"Yeah, pretty cool you're working for that famous photographer now," he said.

"Just a temporary thing. I go back to work with Johnny on Monday," I replied.

"Still, how cool is it to work for her? Was she doing a cover for *Vinyl Vision*?" Howie asked enthusiastically.

"No, not this time. I'm a little tired so I am going to turn in early. It seems like I interrupted something," I said, looking at Sherry. She looked embarrassed and straightened out her blouse.

"No, you didn't interrupt anything," Howie said defensively, "Tell us about your trip."

"Another time. I need to check my answering machine and chill out." I said.

"OK, that sounds good. Sherry and I were just about to go out anyway and get something to eat," Howie said.

"Well, it was nice meeting you," Sherry said.

I went into my room and closed the door.

The red light on my answering machine was blinking. Three messages. I hit playback.

Beep. "Sam, this is Rachel. I heard from Howie's sister that you got a job working for Isadora Teivel. That's so cool. You have to tell Derek and me all about it. How about coming over for dinner when you get back. Give me a call."

Beep. "Sam, this is your mom. How come you never call? Your father is worried about you. I heard from Rachel that you got a big job for some famous photographer and may even be working for National Geographic. Your father and I are so proud of you. I know you're busy but if you can find time in your busy schedule, we would like to hear your voice. I hate answering machines. I hope you get this message. Love, Mom."

Beep. "This is Con Edison to remind you that a bill is due on March 17th. To avoid penalties please send your check before March 17th. Thank you."

I walked out to confront Howie.

"What did you tell your sister?"

"What do you mean?"

"About my new job. I just got a message from my family. They think I have a full-time job with Izzy!"

"Don't you?" Howie responded, shrugging his shoulders.

"NO! It was just for the week. I go back to my regular job on Monday."

"Hey, it's still pretty cool you got to work with her. Mazel Tov!" Howie said cheerily, and he and Sherry Finkelstein from Rosemount left for dinner.

I went back into my room, collapsed onto my futon, and stared at the white stucco ceiling. After a time, I picked up the phone and called Rachel.

"Hi Rachel, I'm back in New York."

"Sam! How did it go? I mean, what is she like? How did you land that job? It's so exciting!"

"Slow down Rach. I think you have been misinformed."

"What do you mean? I heard from Jackie that you landed a gig with Isadora Teivel. She said Howie told her."

"It is partly true but it was just a temporary job and now it's over. I'm back working with Johnny on Monday."

"Oh," she responded.

"What did you tell, Mom?" I asked.

"Did she call?" Rachel said.

"She thinks I am shooting for National Geographic."

"I never said that. She never does get things right."

"I know. Do you remember when you told her you might get a part-time job in the MOMA gift shop and she thought you were going to have and exhibition there?"

We were both laughing now.

"Sam, if you don't have plans today why don't you join Derek and me for dinner. You can tell us all about your adventures."

"That would be great—although I may bore you with my stories. I mean working for National Geographic is not as much fun as people think."

"We'll see you around six. Do you remember where Derek lives?"

"Off Broadway on East 4th Street across from Tower Records. Third Floor."

"That's it," Rachel said.

"Now I only have to call Mom and straighten her out. I hope she's not too disappointed."

I dialed the number.

"Hi Mom. How's Dad?"

"Oh, Sam, it is so good to hear your voice. It's so exciting what Rachel told me about your new job."

"That's one of the reasons I'm calling."

"Is everything OK? Did something bad happen?"

"No, no, everything's fine. I just didn't want you to misinform the neighborhood as to what I'm up to."

"What do you mean? Rachel said you were working for some famous woman at National Geographic."

"First of all, the woman I worked with…"

"Worked with? Did you get fired?"

"It was a temporary job to fill in for a friend, that's all. I'm back to work with Johnny on Monday."

There was silence on the phone.

"You still there?" I asked.

"Yes dear. I am just a little worried since I told Esther next door about your new job, and you know how she gossips."

"Oh, I'm sure you will figure it out," I said. "How's Dad?"

"He went into work today to check some inventory."

"So, what are you doing today?"

"I am cleaning the kitchen and organizing some things."

"Cleaning the kitchen! You haven't cooked in years. What's there to clean?"

"There is always cleaning," she responded. We talked a little longer. I told her I would try to call more often and we hung up.

This would be my first time seeing Derek's loft as we always met outside on the street. I was still contemplating the week and my inner voices were fighting with each other about how much information I should share.

I arrived at an old six-story building on East 4th that was probably built in in the '40's. The front door was made of wood with a large glass window and metal bars. I looked for Derek's name on the buzzer and was surprised to see only six tenants listed, one for each floor. Derek Alan was the third button down. I pushed it and waited.

A voice with an English accent sounded from the speaker, "Is that you, Sam?"

"Yep," I responded.

"I'll come down. The lift is not easy to operate," Derek replied.

A loud sustained buzzer sounded and I could hear the front door unclick. I opened the door and entered the vestibule where I faced an old-fashioned manual elevator, the kind where you pull on a metal handle and slide the scissor gates to the right. I could tell Derek was on his way by the loud engine noise the elevator made on its way down.

"Sam, glad you could make it," Derek said as he slid the door open. "Get in and I'll take you up."

He closed the gate until it clicked and then rotated a handle that was mounted on a copper semi-circle.

"It's old and temperamental but it works," Derek said, acting as if he were the captain of a ship.

We arrived at his floor and, like Johnny's studio, the elevator opened to the entire floor. No wonder Rachel wanted to move here, I thought to myself. The place is enormous.

"Nice space, Derek. How long have you been here?" I said as I stepped into his loft.

"I bought it about 25 years ago when I was making money as an artist. The neighborhood was in really bad shape and it was a pretty good deal. I basically had to gut and rebuild. That's how I learned to do carpentry," Derek said.

Rachel appeared and hugged me.

"Great to see you, Sam! Can I get you a glass of wine or a beer?"

"What have you got?" I said turning to Derek.

"How about a Newcastle Brown Ale at room temperature," Derek suggested.

"That works," I said. I kept looking at the expanse of Derek's loft. It went on and on.

Rachel brought me the bottle of beer and offered to take me on a tour. It was the sort of loft that you see in movies and think to yourself, nobody really lives like that in New York City.

As Rachel took me around, she explained all the changes Derek was planning and how he wanted to get better storage for his paintings and expand the kitchen and construct a back area for a guest room. I was a bit jealous of the space she lived in but also relieved that she finally had found a decent guy. She was always the rebellious one growing up. While I played the part of the dutiful son in middle school, she was out pushing the limits of a conventional high school life. Every couple of months she would bring home a new boyfriend who in her eyes was "the one." She seemed to be attracted to intellectuals who, trying to impress me, would quote Marx, Kierkegaard, or Dylan Thomas. In truth, I could have cared less but I took on the role of the disapproving father, since our father was never around. One boyfriend, Mark Edelstein, gave me a twenty-dollar bill just for, as he put it, "the hell of it." They all ended up as disasters and Rachel would be moody for weeks and retreat to the sunroom, converted into her painting studio. The smell of her oil paints would permeate the house. Periodically she would snap out of her funk and appear with another new boyfriend.

Derek was different. He seemed less self-absorbed and more practical. I could tell he and Rachel were really smitten. Although the relationship was more than a year old, they still appeared to be in the early bloom of love.

"We're having spinach lasagna tonight with a salad," Rachel said.

Derek, wearing a kitchen apron, pulled out the glass Pyrex dish from the oven and placed it on a trivet centered on the refurbished dining room table. Rachel pulled the salad out of the refrigerator.

We all politely took turns dishing onto our plates and Rachel went around the table filling the wine glasses. Finally, she sat down. "So," she said, "What was it like to work with a celebrity photographer?"

"It was interesting," I replied.

"Can you do better than that?" Derek asked.

"OK. She was demanding, disorganized, rude, coked up and mean. Other than that, I had a great time."

They both stared at me and there was a moment of awkward silence. Rachel broke the silence. "That bad?"

"At the time it didn't seem to be."

"Do you think you'll ever work with her again?" Derek asked.

"I'm not sure. I think I did a good job, although Izzy would never say so. I mean, I did what she said and the film looked OK."

"You never got to look at the film?" Rachel asked.

"No, I handed it off to Mark, her real assistant. I suppose I should ask him when I get a chance. He flew to LA this morning to meet up with Izzy."

I began stuffing my mouth with lasagna. "Really good lasagna Rachel. When did you become a chef?"

"Thanks. It's one of Derek's favorite meals. Knowing that you're a vegetarian, he suggested I make it for you. I'm glad you like it." Rachel clasped Derek's hand and gave it a squeeze. "I think it's cool you got to work with her, Sam. Even if you don't ever work with her again. It should help your career and open some doors."

"Derek, how did you get your start as a painter?" I said, trying to move the conversation away from me.

"That's a long story but I always wanted to be an artist ever since I was a kid," Derek said, looking at Rachel and smiling.

"Did you grow up in London and go to the Royal Academy?" I asked.

"No. I am basically self-taught and went to school for a graphic design in Leicester, where I grew up. My parents were from Poland but couldn't go back after the war because of the iron curtain. I did try to get into the Academy but was denied. I think it was my Cockney accent."

"I don't hear a Cockney accent, not exactly Eliza Doolittle," I said.

Derek laughed.

"Well, I'm not sure that's the accent I was referring to but I was told, after being rejected from the Academy, that I would have to speak the Queen's English in order to succeed in the art world. It came in very handy when I arrived in the '60's. Beatlemania was in full throttle and I figured I could ride the wave and it worked."

"Derek is an amazing contemporary conceptual painter," Rachel said. "He is just modest about his work. He was one of the first artists to use bold color and geometric form on canvases."

"You can see my work in the storage area of the loft," Derek said with an ironic smirk.

"Oh, come on, Derek, your agent screwed you and so did the gallery. You'll get your work out there again." Rachel rubbed Derek's back.

"At least I secured this loft from some of the sales," Derek said, sitting up and admiring his domain.

"That's right, sweetheart, you did well, and like the Phoenix, you will rise again." Rachel said this in a childlike voice. The two love birds started bantering with each other and I suddenly felt as if I was no longer in the room. I cleared my throat to get their attention. It was getting late and I needed to get back home. I thanked them for the wonderful meal and company, and we agreed to meet up more often.

Derek took me down on the elevator and walked me to the door.

"I just want to tell you how much I love being with your sister. I don't want you to get the wrong idea, but you should also know that I am married," he said in a whisper.

"What!" I said in disbelief.

"My wife is in Scotland and suffers from acute Parkinson's. Rachel knows and is OK with the situation."

I didn't know how to respond.

"It's a long story and I will fill you in another time, I just wanted you to hear about my wife from me and to know that we are all OK with the current arrangement."

I didn't know what to say to him, other than I could see my sister was happy.

"Thanks for letting me know and if Rachel is OK with it, then so am I," was what I managed. I tried to give Derek a goodbye handshake but he pulled me in for a hug and whispered, "I can't tell you how relieved I am to hear that."

CHAPTER 13

THE OFFER

The weeks flew by and Johnny was too busy to notice Ong was missing. Campbell Soup, MTV, Rolex, and CBS were all knocking on his door. I would get in at 7 AM and usually leave around 7 PM, five to six days a week. As a bonus, Johnny surprised me by giving me a Hasselblad 500C and an 80mm lens, which was a curse and a blessing. The curse was I couldn't afford any of the accessories. The blessing was that I now was the possessor of one of finest cameras ever made. It was the most expensive piece of photo equipment I had ever owned and I felt like a real professional. In short, life was good.

At the end of long week, I was heading out of the studio when the phone rang. Johnny picked up the phone and started talking. I waited to see who the call was from when he held the phone toward me and said, "It's Mark."

Mark? I hadn't heard from him in months.

"What do you think he wants?" I asked.

Johnny, with a deadpan expression, said, "He wants to talk to you."

"Hey Mark, what's up? I haven't heard from you in ages. How are things with Izzy?" I said in my usual upbeat way. I could see Johnny was staring, waiting to see what this was all about.

"Hey bro, how's it going? Good to hear your voice. Sorry I haven't checked in with you for a while. It's been just crazy with all the travel and shoots."

"No problem. It's great to hear from you," I said.

"I'm having a lot of fun. Izzy has softened a bit. But this travel is getting to me and, well, my wife is not happy."

"Sorry to hear that. We're doing great here. Johnny is busy and keeping me busy," I said, waiting to hear the real reason for his call. Johnny was staring at me.

"Sam, the reason I'm calling is I have to stop working with Izzy. My wife says she will leave me if I continue. She's given me an ultimatum. If I don't quit by the end the month, she's walking out on me with our baby."

I looked at Johnny, who raised his eyebrows.

"How can I help, Mark? I'm working with Johnny. I can't just get up and go. He needs me. Besides, I think Izzy hates me."

"Hates you? Hates you? Why do you think that! She keeps talking about you. She's always saying, "If only you were more like Sam. He did this, he did that."

I was stunned. I really thought I had blown it. It took me a week to get the experience of working with her out my system.

"Sam, she wants you to work with her full time," Mark said.

"Look, Mark, I appreciate your thinking of me, but Johnny needs me and we are doing just fine."

"Sam, at least consider this offer. I mean, you would be famous just by association. You would have all your expenses paid, meet celebrities, and you would be able to write your own ticket whenever you stop working with her."

"I don't know, Mark. I need some time to process this. And if I consider the offer, I will need to clear everything with Johnny. It's a lot to think about." I said looking at Johnny as he nodded his head.

"Can you let me know by Monday, bro?"

"Maybe, but I don't think I could start for another month if I even considered the job."

"Sam, if I told my wife and Izzy that I could make this change in a month, that would buy me some time. I got to run. The baby's crying. I will check in with you on Monday, bro."

I held the phone listening to the dial tone and watched Johnny put his head down on the table as if to take a nap. I put the phone on the cradle. "What do you think I should do, Johnny?" I asked.

Johnny lifted his head off the table and said, "What do you want to do?"

"I don't know. I like working here. I think I'm pretty good plus you're great to work for. I mean, we work well together. Izzy is crazy to work for and I don't even think she likes me!"

"Well, she must like something about you. Why would Mark call you and ask you to work for her?"

"I don't know. Maybe Mark is just saying that so he can leave. I mean, if she liked me, she sure didn't show it."

Johnny didn't say anything for a while, which made me feel uncomfortable.

"I think you should take the job," he said suddenly.

"What do you mean?" I replied.

"I mean, YOU SHOULD TAKE THE JOB," Johnny said.

"But what would you do without me? I mean, won't you need a first assistant with all the work that's coming in?"

"Look. I overheard that you would not have to take the job for another month. I could interview and find someone by then. It will be a great opportunity for you to work with such a famous photographer. Plus, you need to spread your wings, man, and get out of this studio and learn more about that type of photography. You've been a great assistant and friend and you will forever be a part of our family. But I need to kick you out of the nest so you can fly." Johnny raised his arms and mimicked flapping wings. I wasn't sure whether to laugh at his gesture or cry.

It took a while to comprehend what Johnny was telling me but I knew he was right.

"What if it doesn't work out? Can I come back and work for you?" I said smiling.

"No way! Anyway, you won't want to come back after working with Izzy."

I took a deep breath. "OK Johnny. I'm going to call Mark tomorrow and tell him I'll take the job."

"Just remember me when you get famous," Johnny said, laying his head back down on the table.

CHAPTER 14

THE BIG TIME

Monday, May 3rd, 1982.

I squeezed myself onto the local #2 train, heading to 23rd Street. A straight shot. I exited onto the platform at 23rd as the 72nd Street A train was rolling in. I placed myself where I thought the door would be and waited for the train to stop. Within four feet of perfection! I pushed myself onto the train, grabbed a hanging strap, and planted myself. I looked around. I wanted to tell everyone that I was on my way to work with Isadora Teivel. I may have scared a few passengers with my grin because when I made eye contact, they looked away and some moved away. No matter. Fame and fortune were calling. Out of my way!

I reached the front door of Izzy's building at 8:50 and rang the buzzer. A female voice responded.

"Yes?"

"It's Sam and I'm ready to work," I said into the intercom.

"OK Sam Ready to Work. I will buzz you in."

I opened the glass door and walked into a dark gray vestibule. I pushed the elevator button and waited. The elevator opened and I bumped into two elderly gentlemen with their arms around each other.

I apologized. "Sorry. Excuse me. I wasn't looking."

"You certainly were not, young man," said one of the men. "You need to be more aware of your surroundings. You could have injured us!"

I stepped back. "Sorry. It's my first day with Isadora Teivel."

"Oh," said the other. "Another young boy toy for Izzy. Let's hope he lasts longer than the last one." They both laughed.

"Good luck, son," said the other man, holding out his hand. "I suppose we will see you more often since our studio is next door. I'm Merce, and this is John, but just call him Cage. We're going out to get a bite— speaking of which, beware of Izzy. Her bite is worse than her bark." They both laughed and walked past me.

I took a deep breath and got in the elevator. Getting out on the third floor, I walked up to room 302 and knocked.

"Hold on, hold on, I am coming," said a voice.

A young woman with short-cropped hair opened the door. Extending her hand, she said, with a Boston accent, "I'm Tiny, Izzy's office manager. You must be Sam. Come in. Izzy won't be here for a couple of hours. I can show you around."

The studio was sparse. It had one pair of Auto Poles supporting a 9-foot roll of Thunder Gray Seamless. There was a small room to the right which Tiny said was the dressing room. The cases of equipment that I had lugged around New Mexico were stacked next to it. Unlike Johnny's studio, which had a smooth white concrete floor, Izzy's studio had a finely polished wood floor. Toward the back of the studio was the office, or as Tiny would call it, "The insane brain station."

"This is where I live," Tiny said, extending her arm to indicate the space. "Files, phone, light box and lunch area."

"The space is very different from my last gig," I said.

"Oh? What was that like?" she asked.

"A lot more photo equipment."

Well Izzy doesn't spend much time here and most of her shoots are on location,"

Tiny said, smiling. "It's pretty peaceful around here when she's gone."

"What am I supposed to do until Izzy arrives?" I asked.

"I'm not sure when she is coming in, so I think you can start by going through all her equipment and making sure it's working. Her next shoot is this Thursday, outside of Chicago. You leave in two days," Tiny said.

"What celebrity are we going to photograph?" I asked, feeling my energy pick up.

"A bunch of feminists planning a march and demanding stuff," Tiny responded. "It's a request from *Life Magazine*. I think some major feminists are going to be there and I suppose they thought a woman photographer like Izzy would be a good fit. I mean, I think Steinem and Friedan will be leading the march. You may get lucky and see some of them taking their bras off to burn."

"Oh boy," I said. "Well, I guess I better get to work and start going through her gear and ..." The phone rang and Tiny went to answer it.

"He's here, uh um, OK, I know, not yet, OK, alright. You sound like shit. Were you up all night again? Don't know. Uh uhh, OK. I'll tell him."

Tiny hung up the phone.

"Izzy wants you to go to the lab and pick up two bricks of film and test a roll. I'll call the limo to pick you up."

"OK. Anything else?" I asked.

"No. She'll be in this afternoon, after lunch with her friend, Bill Queen."

"Bill Queen the fashion photographer?"

"That's the one. I'm not sure who is crazier, Bill or Izzy. They spend a lot of time together driving around doing blow and socializing. "

"Are they a couple?"

Tiny burst out laughing.

"Are you kidding me! Queen is as gay as they come, although I fear one of these days their crazy behavior will crash."

"What do you mean?" I asked.

"I'll tell you another time. The limo should be here soon and I have to put together your agenda for Chicago."

"Cool. I look forward it," I said.

I headed down to the street and waited for the limo. Looking up, I saw a sliver of crisp blue Manhattan sky and took a deep breath.

"Hey, Sammy, how's it going," said Tony, getting out of the limo. "I didn't expect to see you again after that last trip."

"What do mean, Tony? Did Izzy say something about me," I replied in what must have sounded like a paranoid voice.

"No, not at all. In fact, Izzy kind of likes you. It was you who surprised me by saying yes to this job. Most of her frickin' assistants don't last a week. You got balls—though I rather doubt they're as big as Izzy's." Tony opened the door and I sank into the leathery seat.

"To the lab, sir?" Tony asked, turning his head around to look at me.

"To the lab," I said, wondering what I was doing here.

At Duggal Color Labs, I found Baboo seated behind the counter.

"Hi, Mr. Sammy," he said. "How are you and Johnny getting along?"

"I'm not here for Johnny," I said. "I now work for Izzy. Baboo, I thought you worked at that other lab."

Baboo raised his eyebrows and rubbed his chin. "You now work for Izzy and I now work for Mr. Duggal. That's the New York way. So, Mr. Sammy, tell me, what are you here for?"

"Film for Izzy. She had a couple of bricks set aside for a trip we're taking at the end of the week."

"I'll go and see what's there. Be right back," Baboo said.

I looked around the lobby at the other customers. Some were staring out at the limo, no doubt wondering whom it belonged to.

"Here is your film, Mr. Sammy. And best of luck with Izzy." Baboo placed the 2 bricks of 120mm color film on the counter. I picked them up and walked out.

Tony opened the car door and I stepped in as my audience watched.

Back at the studio, I buzzed Tiny to let me in.

"So, when is Izzy coming?" I asked.

"She said around 2 but that can mean anything. She and Bill are known to disappear for days." Just then the phone rang.

"Yes, he's here. Do you want to talk to him? OK. I'll tell him. No, he didn't call. OK. Uh-uh. OK. Right. See you tomorrow." Tiny hung up the phone and turned to me.

"She's out with Bill all day so she said she'll see you tomorrow."

"Great," I said. "I'll just keep busy until then."

"Good plan," Tiny replied.

At noon Tiny came over to see if I was hungry. We ordered sushi and, when it was delivered, sat down together to eat.

"You know, Sam," she said, "Izzy likes to terrify her assistants."

"You don't say," I deadpanned.

"In truth," she continued, "assistants don't last very long. Mark was here for about nine months. Before him was some guy named Fritz who worked for free and lasted about six months."

"How long have you been here?" I asked, taking the sushi out of the bag and spreading out the ginger and wasabi onto the plates Tiny had laid out.

"I started about a year ago, when Fritz was on his way out. Mark came at the right time because Izzy was driving us all crazy about not finding the "right assistant."

"Us? "I asked.

"That's right. You haven't met the rest of the crew. There is Jimmy her agent who has a company called Contemporary Artist, or as we like to call them Contempt. He and his partner represent high-end photographers. Then there is Jahnie who is the publisher of *Vinyl Vision*. He discovered Izzy back in the '60's in Los Angeles. She was attending Cal Arts and sort of pushed herself onto Jahnie when he was first starting the magazine. She wanted to do the photography for him. He agreed and her first photo session was with Janis Joplin. It ended up on the cover of the second issue and, as they say, 'the rest is history.' Jahnie acts like an overprotective father and checks in with Izzy daily."

"Was that who was on the phone earlier?" I asked, inhaling some sushi rolls.

"Probably. He was pissed that Izzy wasn't in the studio today, training you. It is quiet here without her. The other most important person is Sanjeet. He is her accountant. Be nice to him."

"I met him when I dropped off my bill from the New Mexico trip," I said.

Tiny nodded and said, "He is the one who will pay you at the end of the week."

"I thought you said the magazine pays for everything?"

"They pay for all the expenses related to the job. Sanjeet pays for all the other stuff, like you," Tiny said, swirling some wasabi into the plastic cup of soy sauce.

We finished lunch and got back to our respective jobs. I set up the lights to take a portrait and test a roll of film. Tiny grudgingly agreed to be my subject. I had her sit on a tall wooden bar stool and hold a piece of paper with the emulsion number from the film, the f-stop, and shutter speed written down.

"Smile," I said as I took a Polaroid. Tiny stuck out her tongue and crossed her eyes.

"Very sexy," I said. "Would you mind if I took twelve more with film."

"If you must, but I have to get back to work. So, make it fast." Tiny said. She sat uncomfortably on the stool as I snapped away.

"Final frame," I said.

"Good, because my ass is getting sore."

"OK. You are free to go," I said.

Tiny rubbed her rear getting off the stool and went back to her station and back on the phone. I packed up the studio and told Tiny I was going to drop off the roll of film at the lab. She offered to call the limo but I told her I needed to clear my head and take a walk. The elevator arrived and Cage and Merce stepped out. They were with a woman they introduced as Twyla.

"Another choreographer," Cage said.

"So, you lasted a whole day!" Merce said to me.

"Izzy never showed up," I said, shrugging my shoulders.

"Lucky day for you," Cage said, as the three of them turned and walked to their studio.

When I stepped outside, I thought about my conversation with Tiny and wondered how difficult Izzy could actually become. Mark only complained about being away from his family, not about the abusive nature of employment with Izzy. Of course, I had a taste of that out in New Mexico. But how bad could it be? Surely, I could survive a year with a self-absorbed, drug-induced, manic boss.

I dropped off the film and headed back to the studio. By the time I got there I was feeling calm and ready to take on whatever came my way.

At the studio I found a note on the door. EMERGENCY. HAD TO LEAVE. MORE INFO ON MY DESK. TINY. On her desk I found another note. MY CROWN FELL OUT. MUST HAVE BEEN THE CRAB ROLL. I AM OFF TO THE DENTIST. TTFN TINY.

I sat down at Tiny's desk and looked at her notes, trying to gain some insight into this mysterious job I had just taken on. I was expecting to come in and have Izzy greet me and instruct me as to what my role would be. Looking down at Tiny's desk I noticed the itinerary for Thursday's travel. We were to catch the 7:40 am flight to Milwaukee out of JFK, pick up a rental car, and drive to the Holiday Inn in Madison. What I didn't see was a schedule for a return flight. I also noticed that Izzy would be flying first class and I would be flying coach. I also saw numerous notes for Izzy to call Jahnie. They were underscored with the words: VERY IMPORTANT. I was about to get up and put away the studio lights when the phone rang. I answered it. "Isadora Teivel Studio, can I help you."

"Who the fuck is this?" a voice responded.

"Excuse me? May I help you? You have reached the Teivel Photo Studio. This is Sam speaking."

"That's right, Sammy, you work for me. So where is Tiny and why are you answering the phone?"

"Um, Tiny had an emergency. Her crown fell out and she had to go to the dentist," I said.

"Are there any important messages for me? I am going to be out the rest of the day. I am working on some research," Izzy said.

"I just got back but there are some notes next to the phone saying you should call Jahnie and that it is very important."

"Anything else?" she asked.

"Not that I can see," I said.

"You better call Jahnie and tell him I will call him tomorrow. Tell him I am doing some research on … oh … Mel Gibson. I think that is the next cover. Don't tell him anything about this week's photoshoot under any circumstances."

"Why not? "I asked.

"Just don't say anything. Play dumb. Shouldn't be so hard for you. I have to run. I will see you tomorrow bright and early around eleven." The line went dead.

I put the phone down. "Play dumb." What a bitch!

CHAPTER 15

IT'S LIFE!

Tuesday, May 4th, 1982.

I opened the studio door and, with my best impression of a happy person, I said, "Hi Tiny, how's your tooth?" Startled, Tiny spun around in her chair and jumped up.

"Oh, I forgot you were coming in today."

"Wasn't I supposed to be here today?"

"Of course. I am just not used to other people in the studio. One of the perks of my job," Tiny said smiling. "The film clips are on the light table. You may want to look at them. I look like shit but otherwise they look pretty good."

I walked over to the long, narrow light table, switched on the light, and grabbed the magnifying loop to analyze the film clips. "You look pretty good, Tiny. You can use these for your acting career."

"Very funny. You should destroy them," she said.

"So, did you get a new crown?" I asked, cutting the film.

"No. I saved the old crown, so the dentist just re-glued it and told me to come back in a couple of weeks. Any messages while I was gone?" Tiny asked.

"Just Izzy, simultaneously insulting me and instructing me to keep her next assignment a secret from Jahnie. What's that about?"

Tiny turned to me and explained, "The assignment in Wisconsin is for *Life Magazine* and Jahnie gets really jealous when Izzy works for other magazines."

"Can't she work for other magazines?" I asked.

"She can do a certain number of assignments for other magazines each year. It's in her contract with Vinyl, but Jahnie hates that clause. So, when he comes by today just don't say anything."

"When is he coming by," I said.

"I imagine in the late afternoon when Izzy rolls in."

"I thought she was coming in around 11 this morning," I said.

"Ha! Never believe what she says," Tiny said smirking.

"One more question, Tiny. Why are you called Tiny?"

"Because I have tiny tits!" Tiny said, putting her hands over her chest.

"Oh, OK," I said, embarrassed. "Off to work." I turned to look at the film tests.

The morning went by fast. The presence of Tiny in the room kept me in check and prevented me from prying around the studio. The silence was only interrupted by periodic phone calls, most of them coming from Jahnie.

At 11:30 there was still no sign of Izzy.

"What's for lunch today?" I asked, breaking the silence.

"No lunch for me," Tiny said. "I am meeting my brothers and we are going out, so you are on your own. They should be arriving soon."

Almost on cue the door buzzer rang. Tiny jumped up to ring her visitors in. There was then a knock on the door and two men in their twenties burst through the door and picked up Tiny in a mutual bear hug.

"Tiny titties, how is our little sis doing?"

"Put me down, Donny. We have company," Tiny said.

Donny put Tiny down and looked at me.

"Is this the new slave?" he asked, putting out his hand to me. "How ya doing. I'm Donny and this in my brother Danny, and you know Doris, or should I say Tiny T..."

"Stop," Tiny said, putting her hand over Donny's mouth. "This is Sam. He's the new assistant."

"Good luck, Sam the new assistant!" Danny said.

"Thanks. I think," I said.

The three siblings left for lunch, and I wandered over to Tiny's desk to check out the assortment of delivery menus. I decided to order from a Greek Deli called Zorba. Tuna on rye with lettuce, tomato, coleslaw and Thousand Island dressing. I walked to the studio area and started putting away the photo equipment when the phone rang. I ran back to the office to pick up the phone. It was Jahnie, asking if Izzy had arrived.

"No, not yet. Do you want me to have her call you when she arrives?"

"Yes, as soon as she arrives. And by the way, who is this?"

"I'm her new assistant, Sam."

"She goes through assistants faster than Mick goes through lovers. OK. Have her call me ASAP!" He hung up.

I put the phone back in its cradle and the door opened. It was Izzy. She was wearing her standard white Khaki pants and untucked blue work shirt. Her brown hair was pulled back exaggerating her large tortoise shell glasses. She walked toward me, dragging her feet, not saying a thing. She plopped down onto the armchair, throwing her arms to her sides.

"Where's Tiny?" she asked.

"Out to lunch with her brothers. She said she'd be back around 1," I answered.

"What are you doing?" Izzy said, looking at me with the strangest expression on her face.

"I just finished putting away the equipment, getting ready for our trip on Thursday. Oh, and Jahnie just called. He wants you to call him ASAP."

She looked at me for a while as if she wasn't sure who I was.

"I feel like shit! You call Jahnie and tell him I will meet him tomorrow, at his office around 2. I'm going home. I'm not even sure why I came here."

There was a painfully long silence. Finally, Izzy said, "Oh yeah, I came to pick up some blow." She walked into the storage room and disappeared for a while. When she came out there was a little white powder on the tip of her nose. She looked at me, turned around, opened the front door and said, "See you tomorrow." As she closed the door, the buzzer rang. My lunch. I debated with myself whether to call Jahnie. No. That was Tiny's job.

When Tiny arrived, I told her what had happened. She wasn't happy about having to call Jahnie, but she also explained that this was status quo.

"Jahnie gets pissy when Izzy works for other magazines, so he calls her constantly right before the assignment. Izzy could give a shit," she said.

"Why does he put up with it?" I asked.

"They have a very dysfunctional relationship, sort of like my family," Tiny snorted apparently by accident and then went on to say, "They have a need to drive each other crazy. My theory is both of them feel that without each other, the magazine would be a failure. Just a theory. Don't ever repeat this to Izzy or anyone. I think she is seriously thinking of leaving Vinyl and Jahnie knows it." Tiny picked up the phone and dialed Jahnie.

I ate my late lunch, finished packing up the gear, and got the film ready to take to the lab. I told Tiny I would just head home after the lab and be in at 9 the next morning.

Wednesday, May 5th, 1982.

When I was a teenager, I used to spend hours in the cool damp basement of my home in Cleveland leafing through a stack of *Life Magazines*. They were my window to the world. I never imagined I would actually be on an assignment for *Life*.

The next morning I was stoked, arriving at the famous Izzy Teivel studio. Tiny was there to greet me.

"We have a problem," she announced. "Izzy's not picking up her phone and you have to be at the airport in two hours."

"What do you want me to do about it?" I said.

"The limo is coming in about fifteen minutes. Load up the gear. Here are the tickets. Go to Izzy's apartment. Find a way to get in. Get her on the plane." Tiny shoved the tickets in my hand.

"I will do my best," I said. I loaded the seven cases of equipment and baggage onto a cart and headed down to meet the limo. Tony was waiting.

"I am so relieved to see you, Tony. We have a problem."

"Heyyy, nice to see you to Sammy. What's the problem?"

"Izzy has gone missing, and Tiny thinks we'll find her at her apartment."

Tony seemed unfazed and told me this was not the first time Izzy had "a no show". He drove to 86th and West End Ave. I jumped out of the limo, anxiously approached the doorman and explained the situation. He, like Tony, was unfazed and said it's not the first time.

"I need to go with you to her apartment so give me a minute to find someone to watch the front door," he said. Just then Tony entered through the front door.

"You want me to watch the front for you Juan while you go see if we got a corpse," Tony said laughing.

"Hey, Tony, how's it going? Looks like she's at it again!"

"Can we cut the small talk," I said, trying on my new role as the responsible assistant to an erratic superstar. "We have a plane to catch."

"Follow me," Juan said, pulling out a large ring with a lot of keys on it.

We headed up to the 7th floor and walked down the musty hallway, which had a thick floral design rug and was dimly lit by Empire style wall sconces. At the end we came to a single-pane metal door with an atomic starburst peephole. Juan started knocking softly and gradually began to pound.

"Ms. Teivel, Ms. Teivel, are you there? "Juan said, starting with a soft voice. He repeated himself more stridently, and then more stridently still. "Time to use the master key," he said.

He pulled out his key, unlocked the door and opened it a crack. He took a couple of deep breaths and turned to me, "I like to smell the air before I enter the room to see if we've got a dead body on our hands."

"Oh," I responded.

He opened the door a little more and in a polite, hushed tone called out, "Ms. Teivel, are you there? You have a plane to catch and someone is here to fetch you."

Juan opened the door fully and I got my first look into the apartment. It was dark but I could see books and magazines sprawled on the wooden floors. The furniture was right out of a Conran catalog. We made our way to another room where the door was ajar and Juan began sniffing again. "No dead bodies," he announced. He knocked on another door and called out her name.

This time we heard some moaning. And then: "What the fuck is going on? Who's here?"

It was Isadora Teivel.

I opened the door a crack. "Izzy. It's Sam. We have to catch a plane at LaGuardia in an hour and we have to get going now. The limo is downstairs. All I need to do is get your suitcase. Did you pack?"

"Jesus, why didn't you come earlier? Fuck. I need to shower and pack some things. I'll meet you downstairs."

Juan and I went down to the lobby and I settled into an ottoman.

When Izzy appeared, I stood up and took her bag. She looked like she had been up all night. Her clothes were wrinkled. Her hair was a mess.

"Let's go," she said, and we were off.

CHAPTER 16

WOMEN'S RIGHTS

Izzy, slouching in her seat and staring out the window at the detritus of Queens along the BQE, said not another word until we pulled up to the terminal at LaGuardia, at which point, turning to me, she announced, "See you in Springfield." Her door opened, she exited the limo, she disappeared into the building. I was left holding the bags. Literally. Ten of them.

Tony popped opened the trunk and helped me unload the gear onto the curb. He handed me an envelope with my tickets and spending money. He suggested I give the porter $50 so I didn't have to go inside and wait in line with the hoi polloi. "Good luck," he said, and drove off.

I stared at the mound of gear. Noticing a baggage handler, I waved emphatically to get his attention.

"Now you know this is excess baggage and is gonna cost you a lot inside when you check all your bags," the uniformed man said, looking at me sternly and crossing his arms.

That was my cue. I pulled out the fifty and waved it in front of him. "Do you think you can help me?" I said. He grabbed the money and put it in his pocket. "You got your ticket?" he asked. I pulled out the envelope.

The baggage handler ticketed the cases and placed them on the conveyer belt, and I watched them disappear into the terminal, wondering if I would ever see them again. I kept my silver Zero-Haliburton camera case, my backpack containing a brick of film (20 rolls of 120mm film), a pack of Polaroid, my canary yellow Sony Walkman and some of my favorite cassette tapes, a novel and a KitKat to avoid low blood sugar and satisfy my sweet tooth.

At the gate I saw Izzy sitting in a chair, slouched over in her black leather motorcycle jacket, looking at the floor. I sat down next to her.

"Do you think my feet are too big?" she asked.

"Too big for what?" I responded.

"These shoes. I think I need to get a size bigger. What size shoe do you wear?"

"Me?" I said. "Ten. I wear a size ten."

"I need to get some new sneakers. You can have these if they fit. Where is the closest shoe store?"

"Izzy. Our flight leaves in twenty minutes. We will have to find one in Springfield."

"We can go back to Manhattan and catch a later flight. These shoes are too tight. They hurt my feet." She was looking at her feet.

"Izzy. We can't. This is the last flight to Springfield, and we have to be on it to get there on time to cover the event."

"I hate flying. I hate traveling. I hate these shoes!" Izzy said in a monotone voice.

I didn't know how to respond. I was fully expecting her to stomp her feet and throw a conniption fit. Instead, she slouched back down into the seat, let out a gasp and closed her eyes. When the flight attendant made the announcement that first-class passengers could now board the flight to Chicago, Izzy got up and boarded the plane. I remained seated, awaiting the announcement for the steerage passengers.

When I did board, I squeezed my way through the narrow aisle trying not to injure any of the sitting passengers with the heavy silver Zero-Halliburton camera case. Passing Izzy in first class, I looked at her and she turned her head away, conspicuously losing herself in the flight magazine. I continued down the long aisle to the back of the plane and hoisted the camera case into the overhead compartment. Clutching my backpack and contracting my body to avoid contact with the other two passengers in the row, I stuffed myself into the middle seat. I reached into my backpack and pulled out my Walkman and headphones. Placing them on my head, I pushed play. Allison, I know this world is killing you. Oh, Allison, my aim is true ... Thinking, Elvis Costello the Cole Porter of our generation.

In Chicago Izzy was waiting for me at the gate. Strangely, she looked lost. "What next?" she said. I pulled out my ticket and waved it at her. "We have a connecting flight in an hour to Springfield. Gate 43. Follow me." And off we went, traipsing through the busy terminal corridors, with me scanning the signs above for guidance and Izzy trailing behind in my wake.

This initiated a pattern I was to become all too familiar with in the course of my employment with the famous globe-trotting Isadora Teivel. I would pry her out of her dark, depressing apartment to catch a flight; at some point, she would plead for us to take a "later flight"; once on the plane she would ignore me, until we landed. Then like a helpless child she would blurt out, "What next," and I would guide her to the next destination. Rinse and repeat.

At Gate 43, I was not entirely thrilled to discover our next flight was a "puddle jumper," a small, insignificant prop plane used exclusively on routes to small, insignificant places like Springfield, Illinois. There was no first-class section so Izzy was forced to sit next to me— I could tell she wasn't happy with this arrangement. She grabbed the window seat and stared out of the window. She only came out of her trance when the flight attendant asked us if we wanted anything to drink. Boy did she! She ordered a Bloody Mary with the maximum two small bottles of vodka. She sucked it all down and returned to whatever dreamscape she had been visiting. I put on my headphones. *Sometimes I wish that I could stop you from talking. When I hear the silly things that you say I think somebody better put out the big light cause I can't stand to see you this way...*

When we landed in Springfield, I nudged Izzy towards consciousness and we disembarked to the tarmac. I then led Izzy towards the terminal building, above which hung a sign in giant letters, WELCOME TO THE ABRAHAM LINCOLN CAPITAL AIRPORT.

I managed the collection of our luggage and the renting of our car. Remembering New Mexico, I asked—begged? pleaded with?—Izzy to let me drive. Happily, she nodded yes and soon we were on Route 29 South heading to our hotel, with Izzy in the passenger seat staring out the window into what in Abraham Lincoln's day must have been a featureless prairie. I wondered if there had been any wooly bison, roaming about and whatnot.

"Everything OK?" I asked.

She said nothing for a full ten seconds. And then: "What the fuck am I doing here?"

"Izzy. We are in the Land of Lincoln. We are here on assignment for *Life Magazine.*"

"I know that! But this is not my thing. I photograph famous, narcissistic people for the cover of magazines. We party, we have fun and I take their photos. This is a news assignment. I don't know what to shoot."

I wasn't sure what more to say. I mean, she was the show. She was the star. I decided on a cocktail of earnestness, the obvious and bullshit. I looked her in the eye.

"See what you see. Let the action unfold. And take pictures. Photograph the event. Just follow your instincts, Izzy."

She was quiet and I was sure she was going to tell me to fuck off. After what seemed like forever, she breathed in. "OK," she said, and more silence followed. As we pulled up to the hotel, Izzy said, "I'm sure you want to know."

"Know what?" I asked.

"Yeah, I slept with Mick. I was young and probably stoned. It wasn't that special. I did manage to get some great shots of him."

Jesus! I leapt out of the car and looked around for a porter. Never around when you need them. Izzy headed to the reception desk. I wrestled the equipment onto a cart and wheeled it into the lobby. Izzy walked up to me and handed me my key and announced, "The march begins at eight fucking am so let's meet down here at seven. We will just need my camera, film back, and the Norman 200B portable. I'm going to have dinner in my room. I'll see you tomorrow."

The phone rang at 5:30 AM. My wakeup call. I jumped out bed, brushed my teeth, ran cold water on my face and hair, and headed downstairs to the lobby, clumsily navigating all the equipment down the narrow hallway and into the elevator. I flashed on a movie scene I had seen when I was in high school. It was the brilliant 1920's comic actor Harold Lloyd portraying a professional photographer tripping over all his gear.

5:45 AM

I arrived in the lobby and asked the receptionist to call for our car. It arrived at 6 sharp and I stuffed the equipment into the trunk and back seat. I still had time before Izzy came down. I decided to grab breakfast. One thing I had learned about location photography is that you never know when you are going to eat, so you grab a meal when you can.

I felt excited about this day. I was doing news photography. We were going to cover an historic event for *Life Magazine*. My journalism professors would never have believed this. Most of them tried to fail me because I couldn't type fast enough. In truth, photography and not journalism, was my passion. But how to make a living? My photojournalism professor at Kent State University used to ask us, "What is the difference between a large cheese pizza and a career in photography? A large cheese pizza can feed a family of four." Not very encouraging.

Commercial photography bored me. I fantasized about doing photojournalism in a warzone, in the footsteps of Larry Burrows and Dickey Chappelle (both died in combat). But I knew that was out of the question. As the only son of a survivor of the concentration camps, my parents would not be able to bear my living and dying as a combat photographer. Commercial photography would inevitably be my fate. Yet here I was assisting a famous photographer for *Life Magazine*, how cool! I looked at my watch. Oh shit! 7:15 and no sign of Izzy!

I walked into the lobby and looked around. No Izzy. I went to the front desk to ask if they had seen her. The receptionist said no but she would ring her room. No answer. Déjà vu.

"I need to go up to her room and get her. Could you give me her room number?"

"I am sorry, sir, we cannot give room numbers but I can leave a message."

"NO, I need to make sure she is awake. We have to be somewhere at 8. This is an emergency!"

"Sir, I will need to get the manager and see what he can do."

The receptionist picked up the phone and dialed a number. I looked at the clock.

7:30. "Sir, the manager will come down and try to help you. Can you please take a seat till he comes."

"Look, I will give you $20 if you just tell me her room number. You can come with me."

"The manager will be here soon, sir. Please have a seat."

I kept looking at the art deco clock behind the receptionist. 7:30. I couldn't believe it. Panic set in. "Sir, how may I help you?" said a well-groomed man in a lapis suit, wearing a coconut patterned cerulean colored tie.

I was pleading now. "I need to wake up my boss. I don't know what room she is in and we are supposed to be somewhere at eight. It is really important we get there on time or I lose my job!"

"No need to panic, young man. What is your boss's name?"

"Izzy Teivel," I said.

"You mean the photographer?" he said, suddenly less formal.

"Yes. Now can you give me her room number so I can get going?"

"I thought she traveled with a bigger crew. So, what famous person is she photographing?"

"No one famous. Just some women's march. Now can I have her room number? It's getting really late." I looked at the clock. 7:45.

"Oh, I see. You can't tell me. A women's march. Now that is pretty funny. In Springfield." He moved closer to me. "I'll tell you what," he said, whispering in my ear. "You tell me who the celeb is, and perhaps add a little sweetener, and I will give you the key to her room."

"Are you kidding me?" I said in disbelief.

"I could lose my job," he said, walking away.

"OK, OK. Come back. She is photographing ... Bruce Springsteen." I pulled a $20 bill out of my pocket and handed it to him.

"Bruce who?" he said, taking the $20.

"An up-and-coming troubadour. The Bob Dylan of the Jersey Shore. He's going to be VERY BIG. Now, can you give me the keys?"

The asshole walked behind the desk, picked out a key and tossed it to me.

"Room 327."

I ran for the stairway and raced up to the third floor to room 327. I knocked, yelling, "Izzy, Izzy. It's me. Get up. Let me in."

No answer.

"OK. I am going to open the door in ten seconds. 10, 9, 8, 7 . . . 3, 2, 1."

I put the key in the lock and pushed the door in. The room was still dark, the shades were closed. God help me: I sniffed! Then I turned on the light. The place looked like a hurricane had blown through. Furniture was turned over. Magazines were strewn about. On the kitchen countertop were three lines of white residue. I knocked on the closed bedroom door.

"Go away. I'm not here."

"Izzy, we have to get going. It's eight o'clock and you are supposed to cover the march."

"Oh shit! Why didn't you get me up earlier?"

I took a deep breath.

"I'll tell you what. I will meet you down in the lobby." On my way out I made sure to slam the door.

Izzy finally showed up at nine. Looking awful. She barked, "OK, let's go. We are going to the Capitol building."

Amazing! It was like nothing had happened.

I was to learn that, with Izzy, there was real time—the world and the rest of us are condemned to live in—and there was Izzy time. We were now on Izzy time. Fortunately, the Capitol was a two-minute drive away. Unfortunately, Second Street was closed due the march.

Izzy ordered: "Park the car and grab the gear. We'll cover the marchers moving toward the Capitol."

All that preparation I had done the night before was about to pay off. We were going mobile. I pulled out the Hasselblad with a loaded film back and estimated the aperture and f-stop and handed it Izzy. I grabbed the light meter on a string and placed it around my neck and then hung the backpack on one shoulder with the portable strobe pack on the other shoulder.

131

"Ready when you are Izzy," I said.

Izzy looked at me. "You make a pretty good-looking pack mule," she said. I followed behind her as if I were her lost shadow.

When we reached South Second Street, we were stopped by a couple of cops. "And where do you think you're going?" one of them asked.

Izzy reached into her right vest pocket and pulled out a press pass and showed it to him.

"*Life Magazine*?' the cop said.

Izzy nodded.

"Do you have an ID?" the cop asked, and Izzy pulled a license out of her back pocket. The cop looked at it and then at Izzy and then back at the ID.

"Hey Zeke! come over here. You got to check this out," the cop said, waving to another officer.

I was sure they were going to arrest Izzy for all the tickets we had accumulated in New Mexico. The other cop came over and looked at the ID.

"What celebrity are you here to take a photo of?" he asked.

"Can I have my ID back?" Izzy said, with majestic haughtiness. "I have to get to work."

The cop handed it back to her and waved us through onto the street where we ran towards a wall of women marching in our direction, holding up signs and shouting "In ERA. We Trust." Izzy turned to me and said, "Get Ready."

I was ready. As the crowd approached us, I found myself running backwards, holding up the remote flash and handing Izzy freshly loaded camera backs which she handed back to me after the 12 frames were exposed. Then I unloaded the exposed film roll from the camera back, marked it with a letter, and reloaded another camera back, all the while running backwards and dodging the angry crowd. When I had the chance to look up, I saw the determination of the marching woman who were assailed by insults from spectators lining the street. "Go back to the kitchen!" "A woman's place is in the home and in the bedroom!" It was a hot sunny day and I was drenched in sweat. Just when I was teetering from exhaustion, Izzy turned to me and said, "I got the shot. Let's go."

We walked back to the car and drove back to the hotel. It was around noon and we decided to shower up and meet for lunch. I felt my first success. I could tell Izzy was impressed with the way I handled the shoot, like a gold medal Olympic athlete.

When I met up with Izzy in the lobby, she told me she had gotten a call from John at Life and we needed to go directly to the Capitol. Twelve to seventeen of the women had chained themselves to a pillar in the Capitol building in support of the Federal Equal Rights Amendment. "It looks like we are going to have lunch later," Izzy said.

We drove back to the Capitol building and I pulled out the cases of photo equipment and light stands and hauled it all inside while Izzy fanned her credentials to security. As we entered the rotunda of the Capital, I could see the women chained to each other and to a Doric-style column. Izzy turned to me and shouted, "Set up the lights and do it fast. We don't know how long it will last."

As I set up, she walked up to the chained women and talked to them.

I set up four strobe lights connected to two power packs to illuminate the rotunda. Working as quickly as I could, I placed her camera on the tripod and tested the light using the flash metered to determine the f-stop of the scene. Finally, I put the Polaroid back on the camera and did a test. "OK Izzy, ready when you are," I announced proudly.

I could see Izzy going from woman to woman, putting her hand on their shoulders and saying something to each of them. She then walked casually to the tripod, just as I pulled the polaroid to show her the test shot.

"OK ladies. Look defiant," Izzy roared and she started taking shots. After shooting off 2 rolls of film, 24 frames, Izzy announced to the protesters, "Thanks and good luck."

She turned to me. "I am going to walk back to the hotel. When you get back, give me a ring."

"Sounds good," I replied. I waved to the women and then followed Izzy with my eyes. I saw her pridefully stride down the steps of the Capital and walk jauntily toward the revolving doors, disappearing into the dusk. *What a trip*, I thought to myself.

CHAPTER 17

GUN POINT

It wasn't until I turned 13—and after my bar mitzvah—that my father trusted me to operate the cash register. I'd stand behind the counter, while customers, merchandise in hand, would pull out their bills, usually crumpled and greasy, and slide them across to me. I diligently flattened the money on the green linoleum countertop and counted. Then I entered the price of each individual item into the cash register and pushed "Total." A bell would ring as the machine indicated the sum total of the purchase. It was then my job to figure out in my head the amount of change I needed to return. To this day I can add and subtract in my head in a heartbeat, as if my life depended on it.

Only once in all my summers working at my father's store did I get held up at gunpoint. It was the end of the day and my mother had left to go home and prepare dinner. Two customers were in the store, a man and a woman. The woman had just come in; the man had been walking around for quite some time checking out every article of clothing in the place. When the woman exited without purchasing anything, the man came up to the cash register carrying a pair of pants. My father was in the back preparing to lock up for the night. I thought it was odd that the customer hadn't put the pants down on the counter for me to check the price and when I held out my hands to take the pants, he pointed a gun at me and simultaneously put a finger to his lips to tell me not to make a sound. Without saying a word, I opened up the register and took out all the money and put it in a paper bag with the pants. The man grabbed the bag, put the gun away, and walked out the front door. When he was out of sight, I ran to the door and locked it. Then I started yelling. "Dad! Dad! We've been robbed!"

My father came hurrying to the front counter with his unbalanced gait—in the camps he wasn't allowed to wear shoes and resorted to wrapping his feet in newspapers to ward off the winter cold; the consequence had been frostbite. He said to me, with his thick European accent, "Vat do you mean ve've been rubbed?" I must have looked scared because he looked scared.

"Dad, the last customer, he pulled out a gun and I gave him all the money." I felt shame. I felt I had let my dad down. There was a silence that seemed to last forever.

Finally, my dad asked, "Are you OK?"

"NO!" I said and I started crying. "I'm sorry, Dad. I'm sorry. I didn't know what to do. Should we call the police?"

"NO!" my father said emphatically. "Ve vill not tell anyvone vhat happened. Especially not even your mother. It vould be more trouble."

"But Mom will wonder what happened to all the money?" I said. At this my father smiled.

"Not all ze money. Your mother alvays takes vhats in ze register vhen she leaves. If you tell her vhat happened she vill just get upset. Ve vill tell her it vas a quiet afternoon. Alright?"

"Alright" I said.

That was the longest conversation I ever had with my father. My mom used to apologize for his lack of involvement with me and my sister. The store was the only real connection I had with him. Supposedly one day he'd pass it on to me. My sister had no interest in the store, nor was she expected to show any interest. Only when she had a new boyfriend who needed bell-bottom jeans, or a pair of combat boots to protest the Vietnam War, did she make an appearance.

Who was this balding, overweight man with the strange shoes and even stranger accent? When he spoke to me it was invariably in simple declarative sentences. "Move ze pantz to ze front of ze store." "Mark ze prices on ze front of the JOBMEISTER boxes." "Hang ze raincoats on ze back rack and tag ze price on ze right sleeve." I hoped one day he'd go off on a tangent and ask me something about myself. Or tell me something about him.

We had our work routine. My mom would wake me around 7 and I'd stay in bed until I heard her yell from downstairs: "It's late and your father is waiting for you. Get out of bed NOW!!!" Jumping out of bed I threw on some clothes, raced down the stairs, and ate a bowl of cereal, while my mom lectured me about getting up earlier so I wouldn't keep my father waiting. I jumped in the car, still half-asleep, and my father drove us to the store. He was always dressed up to go to work. I imagined this is how he dressed in Poland before the Nazis invaded. He wore a brown suit and a diamond-patterned tie with a monogrammed tie-clip and monogrammed cufflinks. His bulky shoes were always polished. To complete his look, he wore a brown fedora hat. I wore faded bellbottom jeans and an untucked faded blue button-down work shirt.

The ride from our suburban home to the store took about half an hour. Since we never talked, I looked out the window and watched the transition—from Cleveland Heights, an old suburb with a mix of homes, from bungalow to mini-mansions; through Shaker Heights, the wealthy neighbor, where my sister dreamed of living one day and where her boy-friends tended to live, including Adam Glotsky, who always wore a Harvard sweatshirt and spoke in an affected Boston accent. Every time I saw him, he gave me a joint and told me to take a walk so he could be alone with my sister. We drove past Shaker Square—where we would take the Rapid

Transit train downtown during the Christmas Holidays—and onto Lee Road, entering what we called "the danger zone." The red brick one-story houses started looking monotonous and increasingly rundown. By the time we got to Miles Avenue, some of the homes were boarded up. That's where the store was.

When my father bought the store, there were big windows in front that displayed merchandise, but after the windows were broken three times in one month, he decided to board up the front with plywood and paint the words SALE TODAY ON WORK BOOTS, CARHART'S JOBMEISTER, TENTS, and FISHING GEAR.

We arrived and my father pulled out his keys and slid open the gate that protected the glass of the front door. Once inside he turned on the fluorescent lights and turned off the alarm. Occasionally I would accidently trip the alarm and within ten minutes the Cleveland police would arrive, hands on their guns.

The day began with my father giving me a list of mundane tasks to do. Around 11 AM, my mom arrived, which meant lunch was in sight. At noon, my mom would give me an envelope of cash and tell me to go to the bank and make a deposit. On the way back I would stop at a diner called Tommy's and pick up sandwiches. The bank was only two long blocks away, but I was terrified every step of the way. I had a wad of cash and I was sure someone was waiting to rob me. I'd stuff the envelope in my shirt and act half-crazy, thinking that no one would bother to mug a crazy White dude in the middle of the day. When I reached the bank, I breathed a sigh of relief.

Tommy's was around the back of the bank. Everybody there was White and knew me. "Hey Sam, making a lot of money today!" Tommy shouted from the end of the counter. Everyone in the diner looked at me. "Very funny, Tommy, I was hoping you could lend me some money," I replied. Then everyone would look at Tommy, waiting for his response.

"Fat chance. The usual today?" And everyone went back to their burgers and fries.

Tommy was about forty. His hair was prematurely white and he slicked it back, probably with the cooking grease. He always wore a white short-sleeve service shirt, white pants, and a small white sailor's hat. He had served in the navy and had an anchor tattoo on his right bicep. He had an effeminate manner and the fact that he still lived with his mother, Rosie, who also worked at Tommy's, always made me wonder.

Back at the store, once lunch was over, I had four more hours to kill. At 2 PM the mailman arrived. His name was Huston. He was in his fifties and had a distinguished gray beard. He lived in the neighborhood and knew all the characters I would encounter throughout the day. He gave me their backstories, saying things like, "Randolph only had to serve three years in the pen. Got out, stabbed another person, and they threw him back in." Or "Esther got pregnant when she was fourteen. Never knew the father but she's at it again and is about to have her fourth. At least now that she's twenty-one, she can drink." He always had me laughing. He was constantly in therapy, constantly "self-realizing" something. He was perceptive, though. He understood my frustration with my dad, whom he would tease. "So, when you going to talk to your son?" he'd say to him. "The boy needs to know about the birds and bees or something. He's not getting any younger." My dad would look at him and say, "Ve got vork to do, Huston. Leave him alone and let him do ze vork." Huston would look at me and roll his eyes. Once he pulled me aside and said, "Don't give up on him. Someday he'll realize he has a son…"

Please fasten your seatbelts. We will be landing at LaGuardia in twenty minutes.

The announcement jolted me out of my reverie.

Crammed into my seat—Izzy was up front in first class— I would begin my ritual of pulling all the film rolls out of the plastic bag and carefully stretching and tightening the film lead onto the film spool to prevent it from unraveling. I would then seal the rolls with tape and mark each roll with a letter and number, making sure everything correlated to the "shoot sheet." I reached under my seat for my backpack and stuffed everything into it before the flight attendant had a chance to tell me to put my tray up.

Back at LaGuardia, I found Izzy at the baggage claim. She was pacing. I recruited a baggage claim person to corral our luggage and help me pile up the cases and roll them outside to our waiting limo. Izzy jumped into the car while I, the driver, and the baggage claim guy passed the cases from one to another and into the trunk. I held on to my backpack with the shot film and the Zero-Haliburton Aluminum camera case and ducked into the limo.

Izzy was in a fetal position looking out the window. There was an uncomfortable silence on the ride back but I could see that Izzy's attitude changed when we crossed over the bridge into Manhattan. "I am so hungry. Let's go get sushi when we get back to the studio," Izzy said, turning to me with a half-smile.

"Sure, Izzy," I said. She was quiet again, looking out the window, and I was feeling suspicious. Why was she was being so nice to me?

We arrived at the studio and Izzy jumped out of the limo and ran into the building while Tony and I unpacked the trunk.

"Sounds like you two got along," Tony said, handing me a case to put on the collapsible cart.

"Only in the last half hour," I said.

I wrangled the cases onto the elevator and opened the door to the studio. Izzy was there, preparing to leave.

CHAPTER 18

BILLY JOEL CHANGES HIS MIND

"No time for lunch today," Izzy announced. "I have to run up to Vinyl Records. Set up a portrait light for the shoot and buy some fabric. Tiny will fill you in."

"OK," I said as Izzy left the studio.

Inside I asked Tiny, "What's this all about?"

"Billy Joel is coming to the studio tomorrow for a shoot and Izzy wants to set up some sheer fabric as backdrop. You can get the fabric on Canal Street. Here's the address and contact information." Tiny handed me a piece of paper.

"What about lunch?" I said.

"You're on your own. I have too much to do. Go get some Chinese food while you're down there. Oh yeah, you will need to stop by Pearl Paint and pick up some art supplies. Here's the list and some money for a cab."

I grabbed the list and the money and headed out. I decided to take the subway to Canal and save the money for the ride up. On my way downtown, it hit me that I was going to meet Billy Joel. He had made it big in the

'70's with his album "The Foreigner" but I hadn't heard much since. I didn't know a lot about him and wasn't a real fan. I preferred the Talking Heads. But I did know he was pretty famous and I was going to meet him, at least as Izzy's shadow.

When I got back to the studio, Tiny briefed me on the details of the shoot. I was to set up portrait lighting and hang the sheer fabric somehow in front of the gray backdrop and bring out a fan to create movement in the fabric. Easy enough. Joel and his people would arrive around 2 PM. So, I had all evening and morning to figure it out. She told me that Izzy was out for the rest of the day and would be in around noon the next day. I decided to sort out the film from the "chain gang" shoot and get that to the lab so I could review some clip tests and have the rest of the film processed by the next day. I also decided to use messengers to do all the legwork and concentrate on setting up the studio.

This would be the first studio shoot I would set up for Izzy and I felt confident. I wouldn't have to negotiate maps, figure out where we were supposed to be, schlep heavy cases, and be on the run trying to get to the airport on time. I was trained as a studio photographer and liked the fact that it was one location with controlled lighting. It was a bit unnerving to second-guess what Izzy wanted as a portrait light but I remember Mark telling me she was pretty clueless with the technical side of photography, so whatever I did that looked good would go unquestioned. I figured that as long as the strobe lights went off when Izzy pushed the shutter button and an image appeared on the Polaroid that looked decent, it would be OK.

The following morning, I went to the studio and found Tiny on the phone. She was nodding her head and saying, "Uh uhh, uh uhh I will tell him when he gets in. Does Izzy know? OK I will leave a message on her phone."

"Who was that? "I asked, surprising her.

"I didn't hear you come in. That was Joel's agent. It appears Billy was up all night 'creating' and he is too tired to come into the city today for a shoot."

"What does that mean?" I asked.

"Well, this could be a problem. You and Izzy are heading down to Florida this weekend to photograph Ivana Trump and her kid."

"So, what's the problem? We have a couple of days," I said, a little confused.

"The problem is the Ivana shoot is for another magazine and the folks at Vinyl don't know about it. It turns out Billy's agent wants Izzy to come out to his home on Long Island for the shoot and we have to do it before Florida to meet Vinyl's cover deadline."

"We can shoot Thursday and run the film and have it over to them by Friday," I replied.

"Maybe. But that doesn't leave any room for fuck-ups," Tiny said, rubbing her chin, "and there are always fuck-ups."

"Well, I'm ready. We just need to get Izzy out of bed."

"Easier said than done. I have a plan but I need to plant some seeds. Beginning with a message on her answering machine." Tiny picked up the phone.

"Isn't Ivana married to that really crude real estate guy? I asked.

"That's the one."

"What magazine?" I asked.

"I can't tell you right now, only because Vinyl doesn't know about this one," Tiny replied.

"Why not the asshole husband too? I mean why only Ivana and the kid?" I asked.

"The Donald may be there and he might want to be part of the photos, but we won't know till you get there. My, you are full of questions today!" Tiny started dialing.

I stood by to overhear what Tiny was plotting. Oh, she was good! The message she left with the answering service was that Joel really wanted Izzy to come to his place and see his recording studio, his motorcycle, and share in some special treats. Next she called Vinyl to tell them the change of plans and made it sound like it was an exclusive and Joel never lets photographers near his home. She then called someone at the "other magazine" to tell them that Izzy would be in Florida on Saturday. The shoot was scheduled for that Sunday at 3 PM sharp at Mar-a-Lago. Tiny got off the phone.

"Not bad, eh?" she said to me.

"I am impressed. Do you think it will work? And by the way, what is Mar-a-Lago?"

Tiny laughed. "Mar-a-Lago is Trump's estate in Palm Beach. It's as crude as he is. A perfect fit for the photo shoot. As far as my plan working, all I can say is I hope it works for your sake. If it doesn't, she'll blame you."

"Me? I had nothing to do with all this!" I said, putting my hands up.

"You're the low minion on the ladder, so get used taking the blame for everything that goes wrong," Tiny said, adding, "It will all be fine. This is not my first rodeo."

"Not very reassuring, but what do I have to lose?"

"Your job." Tiny said.

"I guess I'll just pack up the equipment and get ready for Long Island."

"That would be a good idea since you leave tomorrow," Tiny replied.

I looked around, admired my studio setup, and started taking it apart. The day went into high gear and Tiny's plan seemed to be working. Izzy took the bait. We decided to pick her up the next day at 11 and head out to the Island.

But things didn't go as planned. Izzy canceled the trip to the Island and managed to get Joel to come into the city. We hauled his motorcycle into the studio on the freight elevator and I reset the shot, draping torn shear material from the ceiling, with a few fans blowing. It made the cover shot. The film came back Friday night while I was packing up the gear for a Saturday morning flight to Florida. It was a long night and an early morning, but this time I figured in an extra hour to pry Izzy out of bed and we made the flight. I was beginning to get the hang of it.

CHAPTER 19

THE KING AND
QUEEN OF KITSCH

As a preadolescent, I often traveled to Coral Gables, Florida, with my mom and sister to visit Grandma Meta. My father would stay in Cleveland to take care of the store.

Grandma Meta was my only grandparent. Other extended family, that I was aware of, were either living in Israel, across the United States, or dead, victims of the Holocaust carried out in Europe during World War II. My maternal grandfather died before I was born and we were forbidden to mingle with our cousins in Cleveland for unknown reasons. Grandma Meta eventually moved in to spend her last years with us. Coming home one day after school, I found my mother with our neighbors sitting quietly and grieving in the living room. When I asked what had happened, my mother told me that Grandma Meta had died. Not knowing how to react, I ran up the stairway to the third floor, crawled out the bathroom window, stepped onto the roof, looked up at the sky, and cried. It was the first death I had ever experienced.

As I stepped off the plane onto the Miami Airport tarmac, the humidity and the scent of gardenias transfixed me for a moment.

"We have to be at Trump's in a couple of hours," Izzy barked at me.

"I'll get the bags and meet you at the rental car pickup," I replied.

All the bags arrived, which cleared the first hurdle. I piled them on a baggage cart and met Izzy at the Hertz counter.

"Here's the contract. Take the shuttle bus and get the car. I will be waiting outside for you. I don't feel like driving today," Izzy said.

Hurdle number two cleared.

The ride to West Palm was pleasant. I drove on 98 East over a long, narrow bridge past Bingham Island onto South Ocean Boulevard to the Mar-a-Lago Club. Izzy was resting her head on her folded arms, propped on the open window of the car door with her hair blowing in the breeze. When we arrived, we were greeted by a Hispanic woman who told us to wait in the lobby.

"Ivana will be right out. She is running a little late today."

We both looked around the ornate lobby. An excess of marble, gold leaf, chandeliers, and oriental rugs, adorned with large Flemish tapestries, similar to ones I had seen at the Cloisters in Fort Tryon Park in New York.

"Posh," I said, turning to Izzy.

"Very," she replied. "Only it's fake."

"Any idea where you're going to shoot?" I asked.

Izzy looked at me. "The lobby works for me. I just want to get this over with so we can go to the hotel."

"I'll get the lights."

Ivana came out to greet us with her son, Donald Junior. She was dressed in a white gown and wearing diamond studs. Little Donald reminded me of the Gainsborough painting "The Blue Boy." He was wearing blue silk knickers with knee-high white stockings, and a white ruffled shirt. He was about 8 years old.

Ivana extended her hand to Izzy and said in her European accent, "Vell hello, Izzy. It is nice to meet you. I am a big fan of your vork. Donny and I are looking forward to having you take our portrait. Zhis is Donny Junior and ve vould also like for him to be in ze voto."

"Sure," Izzy said, smiling.

"And who is zis young man?" Ivana said, looking at me.

"This is Sam. He is assisting me today."

Ivana extended her hand to me and for some insane reason I took it and ritualistically kissed it. "It is a pleasure to meet you," I said. Everyone was startled, including myself. Izzy rolled her eyes at me and Ivana stepped back. "Vat a sveet boy," she said.

I couldn't believe I did that. I had seen it in so many films. Maybe Izzy would fire me and that will be that. I could get back to a normal life.

To break the awkwardness, I said I would set up the lights.

When I came back to the lobby, Izzy was sitting on the red crushed velvet couch with Ivana. Donny Junior was off with the nanny.

"Excuse me, Izzy. Where would you like me to set up the lights?" They both looked up at me.

"Right here. I want to photograph the family sitting on this couch. Ivana, what time is Donald showing up?"

"He vill be here soon. He's out at ze club talking business or some zing. He never stops vorking, that man. So full of ideas."

I set up the portrait lights and some auxiliary lights to illuminate the ornate background. Just as I was about to load the film back, I heard a booming voice from behind.

"Ivana, my love, I am so sorry I'm late. I was meeting with some new clients about a property I'm interested in. Did I miss the photo?"

"No, not at all, Donny. This is Izzy and ve have had a lovely chat about zhis and zhat. I think ve are almost ready for the shoot, isn't that right, Izzy?"

Izzy looked at me and I gave her a thumbs up.

"About ready. We just need to find your son."

"Donny, Donny. Come here sveetie. Ve are ready for ze voto."

"I only have about five minutes, then I have to get back to this meeting, Izzy, so make it quick," Trump said in a brusque manner.

I could tell Izzy was not happy with his order and wondered how she would respond. She looked at me and asked if the camera was ready and I nodded my head.

"OK, now I want Donald standing behind Ivana, and Ivana, you are sitting on the red couch and little Donny is sitting on your lap."

This was to be one of the most formal portraits I had ever seen Izzy take and I wondered what she was up to. Everyone did as they were told.

"OK. Is everyone ready? Look here."

Izzy took one photo and said, "OK, perfect. That's it."

Donald looked startled. "How do you expect to get a great shot of me by only taking one picture?" he asked.

"You only have five minutes, so I'll take my chances," Izzy responded.

"No, no, no. That's a huge mistake. What if someone had their eyes closed?"

"Then one of you will look like you're sleeping," Izzy said.

"OK, OK. How much time do you need?" Trump asked.

"Twenty minutes and total control," Izzy said.

Trump looked at her and smiled.

"I like you. You're a good negotiator. Not as good as me but you have… chutzpa. Is that how your people say it?"

"My people?" Izzy asked.

"You know what I mean," Trump said. "Let's get started. You now have nineteen minutes."

Izzy went into action and got the trio to look ridiculous without them knowing it. It was at that point that I realized her genius as a portrait artist. It wasn't so much about the lighting, the composition, or any of the formal elements of portrait photography. It was how she took control of her subjects and had them submit to any whim she could imagine—the more provocative the better. Her gift? Setting her subjects free. From what? From the burdens, the clichés, the prison house of their celebrity. And to what end? The aggrandizement of her own celebrity!

A happy thought emerged from my mind, me, a nobody from Cleveland, was the assistant to a genuine American genius!

CHAPTER 20

MARK GETS DARK

There was lull in the schedule for about a week. Izzy had decided to travel south to the Virgin Islands where her family had a home. Her dad had been in the Air Force and Izzy had grown up moving from base to base, which perhaps explained her ease in living like a nomad.

It was Friday afternoon, and I was about to leave the studio when Tiny yelled out, "It's Mark on the phone and he wants to talk to you." I took the phone from Tiny.

"Hi Mark, what's up?"

"Hey Sam, long time. If you don't have plans for tonight, I thought we could go out and catch up."

"I never have plans, Sam. I lost my social life when I started working for Izzy."

"There's a club down in Tribeca that just opened up and I thought we could check it out. We could meet at the Westend Bar around 7:30, get a few drinks, and head on down."

"That would be great, but what about your wife and baby?"

"The baby is too young to go to the club."

"Yuk."

"No, they are out of town. Erin took the baby to see her sister in Jersey so I'm a free man this weekend."

"Cool. I'll see you at the Westend and we can go from there."

As soon as I hung up the phone Tiny looked up at me and asked, "How's Mark doing? I haven't heard from him since he left working here."

"He's seems OK. I just think he was a bit traumatized by working with Izzy and stays his distance," I responded.

"They left on pretty good terms," Tiny said.

I realized that was probably the wrong thing to say so I quickly added, "He's also really busy working as a full-time photographer. I think he's now working as a freelancer for *People*. Anyway, I will let you know on Monday. Got to run. Have a good weekend, Tiny," I said, walking away.

"You too. Remember, even if Izzy is out of the studio, you still have to show up on Monday. There is a list of things you have to do," Tiny said as I walked out the door.

It was one those gray February days in Manhattan where the chill from the Hudson River penetrates your clothes and gets into your bones. Growing up in Cleveland prepared me for that chill. It was called the "Lake Effect." The warmth of Florida still lingered in my body, so the chill seemed more intense than usual. Walking toward the subway, I realized it was Friday the 14th, Valentine's Day. I was so out of sync with the calendar that it wasn't until I saw cupids and heart cutouts in the local bookstore window that I put it together. Suddenly I was surrounded by men carrying freshly cut flowers and couples walking arm and arm.

Opening the door to my apartment, I was expecting to see my roommate on the couch but to my surprise he was gone. There was a note on the dining table that said, Went with my girlfriend to Long Island to meet her parents. Will be back Sunday evening—Howie.

The weekend was looking better and better. I showered and dressed in the hopes of finding my Valentine tonight. It was 7:30 when I got to the Westend and, just like the year before, Mark was sitting at the bar chumming it up with some other single guys.

"Hey, Sammy, how are you doing?" Mark got up from his bar stool and gave me a big hug. "Let me buy you a drink." Mark had a big smile on his face. "So, how's Izzy treating you? Are you ready to quit?"

"Not at all. I think I am actually getting the hang of it."

"Just watch out. If she finds out you like the job, she'll make your life even more miserable."

"Well, Mark, what have you been up to? Tiny was wondering why you never stop by?"

"I have been busy, shooting a lot and of course the family stuff. Besides, I haven't got Izzy out my system yet. I still feel nauseous when I think about her." Mark gestured to the bartender and ordered two beers.

We drank our beers and I listened to Mark tell me about his assignments with *People*. I was a bit jealous and feeling that I should be shooting rather than assisting. I also knew I had a ways to go before even thinking about starting my own business. We paid the tab and headed to the 72nd Street subway station to go downtown to Tribeca.

As we walked onto the platform, it occurred to me that we looked like a couple going on a Valentine date. We were both wearing blue jeans and jean jackets with our collars up. Mark was Daryl Hall and I was John Oats without the mustache. It didn't matter. It was nice to be with Mark again and I owed him a lot. He was the big brother I never had. A comrade for life.

"So, what is this club about?" I asked as we both plopped down on some available seats.

"I heard about it from one of the editors at *People*. It's a club for breakers."

"Breakers?"

"A type of dance that's becoming popular in the Black and Puerto Rican communities in the Bronx. There will be a lot of B-Boys performing. And it's rumored that Chaka Chan will be singing tonight."

"So can we get in?"

At that point Mark tugged on the lanyard around his neck and pulled out a press pass with his picture. Underneath, in bold letters, it read *People Magazine*.

"We are both reporters tonight," Mark said smiling.

We got off the train at Varick Street and walked east. It was dark and the temperature had dropped. Although we looked good in our denim, I was wishing I had worn something a little warmer. There was long line of people waiting to get into the club. Mark walked up to the front of the line, pulled out his *People* ID and showed it to the bouncer. He looked at us from head to toe, turned to his steroid buddy who nodded, and they let us in. I was feeling the buzz of importance as we strutted into the club, even under false pretenses. The music was ear-splitting with a serious pounding bass beat that vibrated throughout my body. The place was packed, shoulder to shoulder. As we pushed our way in, there were pockets of open spaces. Mark, always resourceful, handed me some earplugs. As we got closer to the open space, I could see dancers spinning on the floor on cardboard, their bodies undulating as if they were possessed, and moving as if they were made of rubber. The crowd was into it, clapping and yelling as the dancers continued to defy physics. It was then that I noticed that Mark and I were among a handful of the White folks in the crowd. My initial reaction was, "Great. Two White gay guys trying to be brothers." Then I realized no one cared. Once my paranoia subsided, I started to pulsate with the rest of the crowd and was in awe of the B-Boys.

Mark managed to find a couple of drinks and just as he handed me a shot of something an announcement was made, and the music abruptly stopped.

"We are now proud to present the one and only Grammy award–winning, Warner Brothers' recording artist, the Queen of Funk, Chaka Khan, singing her new hit, 'Clouds.'"

The crowd went crazy. All spotlights pointed to a small stage and a red curtain parted. Out stepped the Queen of Funk dressed in a Native American bejeweled outfit showing off her midriff. The noise level was painful until Chaka waved everyone to quiet down.

"It's good to be here and I would like to sing my newest song, 'Clouds,' dedicated to the B-Boys and B-Girls in the audience. Let's give them a round of applause."

The music started to pulsate and Ms. Khan pulled the microphone off the stand. She started to mouth the words to her song. It didn't matter that she was just mouthing the words, she was a spectacle, and the crowd loved her. When the song ended, she disappeared as quickly as she had appeared, and the crowd went back to cheering the break dancers. Mark shouted in my ear, "Let's go."

We managed to get to the exit and stepped outside into the cold air. Mark said, "How about coming over to my apartment for a nightcap."

"Sure," I said and we jumped on the train to the Upper Eastside.

It was a relief to go underground and get away from the freezing wind. It appeared half of New York had the same idea. The station was packed, all waiting for the next uptown train. I looked at Mark and could tell by his bloodshot eyes and placid gaze that he had probably drunk one— or ten—too many. The train arrived and, like herded sheep, we all crowded in. We looked for a place to stand and a strap to hold and tried not to look into each other's eyes.

"This is our stop," Mark said. I squeezed out the door, barely fitting through before the doors snapped shut. I followed Mark up the stairs and back into the cold. I saw that he was weaving as we walked east to 83rd Street. He stopped abruptly and pointed to an old brownstone. "I am on the fourth floor. It's a walk up."

As we walked up the narrow staircase, I could see that the building had been neglected. The paint was peeling, the banister was seriously worn, and each floor had a strong stale scent. Mark pulled out his keys and unlocked three deadbolt locks. I had never been to Mark's apartment and, being a family man, I expected to see everything tidy and organized. To my surprise the apartment was a mess, with piles of dirty dishes in the sink and clothes thrown around the floor.

"Looks like a tornado went through," I said.

"Oh, yeah, it's a bit messy. I've been busy, and with Valerie and Erin on vacation and all. Well, you know. What do you want to drink?"

How about some warm tea?" I said, pretending to shiver.

"How about some warm tea with whisky," Mark smiled.

"Sure. Easy on the whiskey. I'm a lightweight."

I watched as Mark poured a little Jack Daniels into my cup and then poured a half cup for himself.

"I think I'll have mine without the tea," Mark said, slamming down the whisky and wiping his mouth with his sleeve.

"So where is Erin?" I asked.

"Sit down and I will fill you in," Mark said. His voice was ominous.

"OK." I sat down at the round oak table, moving some dishes aside.

Mark poured more whisky into his cup and sat down.

"Remember I told you she went on vacation," he said, looking down at the table.

"Yeah, hopefully somewhere warm," I said.

Mark raised his head, he was teary-eyed.

"She took Grace and went to stay at her mother's house in Jersey."

"Not a very warm climate," I joked.

"She left me, Sam! Said she couldn't take it anymore, me being away all the time. I tried to tell her I was just doing it for the family. She said it was too hard being a single parent. I was just trying to get my career going."

Mark finished off his whiskey.

"Wow, man. That's tough. I'm sure she'll be back though."

"No. It's not the first time she left me, but I think it's the last." Mark jumped out of his chair and stared to pace around. "I mean I was just trying to be a good father. I bought them gifts when I had the money. I was under pressure too with my work. But she just wouldn't listen." Mark started kicking the clothes on the floor. "I provided them food and shelter. I mean I was being the best father I knew how to be."

Mark turned to me, his tears flowing now. I stood up suddenly and walked toward him, not knowing what to say or do to calm him down. I blurted out, "I'm sure you did your best and I am sure she will be back. We're all under a lot of stress. Just give it some time, Mark, she'll be back."

Mark looked at me and walked toward the table calmly. For a moment I thought his anger had subsided. Then he picked up the Jack Daniels bottle and swallowed the remaining whisky and threw the bottle against the wall.

"I fucked up! I fucked up! Erin found out I was having an affair with my assistant. We only screwed a couple of times and she meant nothing to me. I was just lonely." He looked at me and I could see the desperation in face. What happened next scared me.

Mark began to calm down and catch his breath. He walked slowly toward a mirror that was hanging by the front door. Staring into the mirror, he said, "She meant nothing to me. I thought Erin was out of town. She was at her sisters in Jersey. I came back from a job and my assistant and I were unloading the gear."

Mark kept staring into the mirror.

"I pulled out some coke and we had a little celebration party. We were both exhausted and the coke kicked in and made me feel fearless. I pulled her into me and we started kissing. One thing led to another and the next thing we're both on the floor." Mark looked down at the floor as if to show me where this had all occurred. He looked back at the mirror.

"The front door must have opened and the next thing I hear is Erin screaming at me to get the fuck out. GET THE FUCK OUT."

Mark put his head down and suddenly raised his right fist and punched the mirror. It shattered. His hand was bleeding and I jumped up and rushed toward him before he could punch the mirror again. I wrestled him to the ground.

"What the fuck are you doing?" I screamed, holding his arms down. My tackle startled him and snapped him out of his rage.

He looked at me with a blank stare. "What am I going to do? What am I going to do? I want to see my daughter again. I don't want to lose Erin."

I let go of his arms and rolled onto my back. We both lay there staring at the ceiling. I said, "Tell her you're sorry. Maybe she'll forgive you."

Mark didn't reply. He didn't move. I don't think he felt the glass shards embedded in his hand. I got up and went to the kitchen to get some towels and wipe up the blood. The explosion of anger seemed to have taken all the energy out of him. He just lay there, tears rolling down his face.

I did what I could to clean him up and walked him into his bedroom and put him into his bed. I felt I should stick around to make sure he didn't hurt himself again and decided to crash on his couch. As I walked out of his bedroom, I could hear him moaning, "The room is spinning and I don't feel so good."

I ran back into his room, grabbed Mark out of bed and dragged him to the bathroom. He retched for what seemed like forever. When he stopped, I helped him to his feet. He seemed to perk up and after washing his face he turned to me and said, "Thanks man, you're a true friend."

"I going to crash on your couch Mark. I'm too exhausted to head home."

"That's cool. I'll treat you to breakfast tomorrow morning. I'm feeling a little better," Mark said, suddenly smiling.

I woke up the next morning wondering where I was. I looked around and suddenly remembered. The apartment looked even worse in daylight. I walked into Mark's bedroom and found him sound asleep. I decided to head out and I left him a note. *Mark, call me when you get up. I had to go home and shower up for the day. Sam.*

CHAPTER 21

JOHN AND YOKO

I decided to cross the park. For me, Central Park has always been a place to escape the stress of the Manhattan grid. The park functions as therapy and after Mark's meltdown, I needed to rebalance myself. The vision of Olmsted in creating the park was openness and equality. The park acts as the antithesis of the city grid that represents capitalism, busy intersections, and efficiency. Intentionally Olmstead designed the park with no center, allowing a person to wander, lost in thought.

I walked with camera in hand, looking instinctively for the rhythms of movement. Sundays were the best days to capture those moments, when the Park was a rush of activity; people on roller skates moving at high speed, weaving slalom down a line of orange pylons; jazz bands riffing on Charlie Parker songs with the hope that a random listener will drop a dollar in a box marked for donations.

That was what most people saw. What I looked for were moments away from the spectacles. The reaction of the crowd in anticipation of a skater crashing, a young couple kissing or engaged in a heated argument while the jazz music played in the background. One thing I learned from Izzy was to "look the other way." If everyone is photographing in the same direction, turn or twist your perspective. The photographs that matter are the photographs that people don't see.

I took my time crossing the Great Lawn and making my way to the West Side. Arriving at my exit on 72nd Street, I snapped out of my park mediation and came out onto Central Park West by the Dakota apartment building. It was a grand ornate structure with a mysterious entrance gate. I had been told *Rosemary's Baby* was filmed here.

As I walked by, I noticed two people lying in wait for someone. One was a nondescript pudgy guy. Maybe twenty years old. The other was a man with a camera and a manila envelope under his arm. I thought he might be a paparazzi waiting for some celebrity to appear. I asked him who he was waiting for. At first, he ignored me and then I showed him my camera. "I'm also a photographer," I said, trying to soften him a bit so he would let me in on his secret rendezvous. He relented.

"I am waiting for John and Yoko. I have some photos I took of them that they said they would sign." He spoke with a Scottish accent.

"Wow, not bad," I said. "Would you mind if I hung out with you and maybe took a few photos?"

"If you don't get in the way and maybe get a few photos of me with John and Yoko?"

"Sure, that would be great." I said.

We waited quietly for a while, and I started to think this guy was probably making up the story. But then the gate opened and there stood John and Yoko. My new friend pulled out the manila envelope and photos.

"Here are the photos to sign, thank you so much, Mr. Lennon and Ms. Ono," he said and he handed John a pen.

John looked up at me and asked, "Who's he?"

"Oh, he's a friend of mine and said he would take some photos of the three of us. Is that OK with you?"

"I guess, but we're in a hurry, mate."

I stayed quiet and began to snap away. A minute later, the two of them stepped into their limo.

"Well, that was cool and unexpected," I said.

"Did you get some good pics?" he asked.

"I think so. I suppose we should trade numbers so I can send them to you."

"Right. Here's my card. If you get some good shots send them here. I got to run.

See you later."

I looked down at the card. Harry Benson, Time Life photographer. *Wow*, I thought. *So that was the famous Harry Benson.* I looked over to the young pudgy guy with glasses who had been silently observing us. He was carrying a paperback book with a worn red cover that I recognized. *The Catcher in the Rye.* Our eyes met. He looked away.

CHΛPTER 22

DUSTIN PAYS A VISIT

"Good morning, Tiny. Have a good weekend?"

"Not bad. Went to CBGB's and saw this band called Blondie. The lead singer was smokin'."

"Sorry I missed it. So, what's happening this week? Any traveling?"

"Izzy left a note for you that she wanted you to start pulling these images from her archive and then take them to the lab to make 8- x 10-inch work prints."

Tiny handed me a sheet of paper with the names of famous people Izzy had photographed.

"What's this about and anyway shouldn't you be on it?" I said, looking at the list.

"She's putting together a book and I have better things to do." Tiny turned away and stared at the calendar on her desk. "She does have a big shoot in the studio on Friday for *Vinyl* and wants to have these images printed up by tomorrow. So, get busy."

"Are you going to tell me who is coming by this Friday or am I going to have to guess?" I tried to see what was written on the calendar. Tiny looked up at me. "Dustin Hoffman."

"Seriously?" I said.

"Seriously," she said. "He's between films and Jahnie met him at a party last week. Someone convinced him to have his portrait taken by Izzy,"

"Benjamin from *The Graduate* for fuck's sake! Great movie!"

"Personally, my favorite was *Kramer vs. Kramer*. Nailed the divorced dad and I should know."

"OK," I said. "I'll track down these chromes and get prints made. Is Izzy coming in today?"

"Nope. Not till tomorrow. She's off on one her lost weekends. Probably see her on the side of some milk carton one day." Tiny let out an unexpected snort.

Izzy didn't show up until Wednesday afternoon and Tiny was not happy. The phone never stopped ringing. Jahnie was freaking out, wondering what had happened to Izzy. He was responsible for getting Hoffman to the studio that Friday and, according to Tiny, was having doubts. Tiny began to panic.

When Izzy entered the studio on Wednesday, Tiny jumped out of her seat. "Where the fuck have you been? Jahnie's been calling for the past two days!"

Izzy looked at her for a moment. "Excuse me?"

Tiny stopped short and began apologizing. "Sorry. That didn't come out right. It's just that Jahnie is driving me crazy ... um ... did you have a fun weekend?"

She was good, I thought to myself. Izzy looked at me. "Do you have the prints for me?"

"Yes, they were done on Tuesday. I'll get them for you."

I handed the folder of prints off to Izzy and she started to leaf through them.

"I need to have a space on the floor to put all these prints down. Tiny, any shoots this week?"

Tiny looked up from her desk and said, "Dustin Hoffman is coming by on Friday. It's a cover shoot for Vinyl. Didn't Jahnie tell you?"

"No. I mean yes. I mean, maybe. I don't remember. That's bad timing. Can we reschedule?"

"It's too late. Jahnie said it's for the next cover, and Hoffman starts shooting another film on Monday. Something about cross-dressing. Anyway, it can't be changed. Besides, you don't have anything going on this week."

"I have to start working on my book. The publisher is on my case to show some work," Izzy said.

"After this shoot I will clear your calendar. It can't be changed," Tiny said.

Izzy stood there quietly deciding how to respond as Tiny and I held our breath.

"OK. But I want to start working on the book now. Sam, take all these images and place them on the floor. I'm going out to see some friends and will be back tomorrow."

"What type of lighting do you want for Hoffman?" I asked in my sincerest voice.

"Just some simple portrait lighting. Set it up today and I will let you know tomorrow if it looks right." Izzy turned around and walked out the door.

"Where do you think she is going?" I asked Tiny.

"I'm not sure but at least she showed up. I'm going to call Jahnie to tell him we've had a sighting and should be good for Friday."

"I guess I'll lay out all these images and set up some lights," I responded.

I spent the rest of the afternoon carefully placing around 200 prints of her iconic images on the glossy wood floor. Looking at them I realized Izzy had been a very busy photographer and had photographed everybody who is anybody in the film and music business. At the end of the day, I set up a simple portrait light and used Tiny as my test subject.

"I'll take this film to the lab and see you tomorrow Tiny. I hope she shows up," I said, putting my coat on and heading for the door.

"I do too Sam. I do too."

Thursday, I picked up the film clips from the lab and headed to the studio. Everything was as I had left it. The color prints were all laid on the floor, the simple lighting portrait set up with the final Polaroid was still taped to the tripod, and Tiny was on the phone.

"No, she's not in yet but it's early, Jahnie. You know she'll roll in around noon. She'll show up. She probably left her phone off the hook … OK, I will call you when she gets in." Tiny slammed the phone down. "What an ass!"

"Jahnie, Izzy or me?" I said.

"Jahnie. He's been calling nonstop. He's so paranoid." Tiny wrote something down on her yellow legal pad.

"You think it's the coke he's been snorting?" I said, putting the film clips on the light table and turning on the light.

"It's Izzie. A lot is riding on this shoot and Jahnie set it up, so if something screws up, it's on his shoulders," Tiny said as she continued to write.

"She'll show up. I mean, has she ever missed a shoot?" I said, looking through the magnifying loop at the film clips, admiring my work.

"If she doesn't show up by one today, you're going to have to take a trip to her apartment," Tiny responded.

The morning went fast and no sign of Izzy. Tiny looked at me. "We'll give her till one then you head out." As we went back to our stations, the door opened.

"Izzy! You're alive!" Tiny said, standing up to greet her.

"What's going on here? What are all my photos doing on the floor?" Izzy said, looking at me with a scowl.

My stomach gurgled.

"You asked me earlier in the week to help you put your book together."

"Oh, yeah, I did, didn't I?" Izzy said and nonchalantly walked toward Tiny.

"What's on the schedule this week, Tiny?"

"Well, you have a photo session with Dustin Hoffman tomorrow. It's a cover shoot. Jahnie's been calling nonstop checking in to see if you would show up and your mother called and said you should give her a call, said you haven't called her in a while and wanted to be sure you were OK … and to remind you that you promised to take your sister to Cats. The other magazine called and asked if you looked at the contract. That's about it for now," Tiny said.

Izzy walked slowly toward the plush chaise chair and plopped down. Tiny and I looked in silence at each other. I strolled toward the light table, switched on the light and broke the silence.

"I have the film test here for you to look at for the Hoffman shoot."

Izzy raised her eyebrows and looked at me as if I were speaking a foreign language.

"Can we cancel Hoffman?" she asked, looking at Tiny.

Tiny jumped out of her seat. "NO! Jahnie would kill you if you bailed."

Izzy looked around the studio as if she had lost something.

"OK. But I need to work on picking the images for the book."

She got up off the chaise and walked over to the light table and looked at the clips.

"This looks fine. What time does Dustin show up tomorrow?"

"11 AM," Tiny said.

"OK. I'm meeting a friend in an hour. I'll be back later tonight to go over these prints. Call my mom. Tell her I am fine and get three tickets to Cats for next week."

"Why three tickets? "Tiny asked.

Izzy smiled at me. "Because Sam is joining us."

"Wait," I said. "Why do you want me to come?"

"Cause my sister needs a date," Izzy said, and she walked out the door.

"Why does her sister need a date?" I said, looking at Tiny.

"How the fuck should I know. I can't believe she left again. Now I have to call Jahnie and tell him we've had another sighting, but it didn't last long."

Tiny picked up the phone and I could hear Jahnie screaming. Tiny placed the phone an arm's length from her ear. After she hung up, I asked her, "What's the deal with the contract from the magazine?"

"I can't tell you much, just that there's a publication that wants exclusive rights to Izzy."

"Does Jahnie know?"

"No and he never will unless Izzy decides to sign the contract and if she does the whole world will hear. That's all I can say for now."

"OK. I'm pretty set for tomorrow. I'll load up the film backs, set up the camera, and head out early, unless you need me to do something."

Tiny looked up at me. "Can you buy me a gun?"

"Seriously?" I asked.

"Just a thought. I'll see you tomorrow."

I woke up realizing I would be meeting one of my favorite actors. Typically, I'm not star-struck but Dustin Hoffman was something different. Seeing *The Graduate* sent my twelve-year old's hormones racing. Then two years later, his transformation into Ratso Rizzo blew me away. How could the same actor become both those people?

I jumped out of bed and opened my bedroom door. Howie was sitting at the table spooning some cereal and reading a thick book.

"Howie. I haven't seen you in while. Where've you been?"

"I've been staying at my girlfriend's apartment a lot. She lives closer to Columbia so it's an easier commute. How is it going? What's it like to be working with the famous photographer?"

"Not too bad. She's a bit erratic but I get to meet some pretty cool people." I said, waiting for him to ask, "Like who?"

"Like whom?" Howie asked.

"Well, today she's shooting Dustin Hoffman at the studio."

"No shit? Can you get an autograph for me?"

"Don't know, but I'll see."

"I mean he is really famous. Good thing he didn't go into plastics." Howie said, admiring his own wit.

"Yeah," I said. "I'm going to get breakfast at the diner but if you're home tonight I'll let you know how it went."

"OK. Give Dustin my best. Tell him I didn't see him at Temple last week," Howie said as I closed the door.

I didn't try to conceal my excitement at meeting Dustin Hoffman. The rest of the commuters on the train must have thought I had taken some ecstasy or mushrooms. I couldn't stop smiling. However, when I arrived at the studio and opened the door, all the air was released from my "happy balloon." On the studio floor were all the prints I had laid out and, in the middle, face down, asleep, was Izzy.

I walked up to the lifeless body and stared down wondering if she was alive. To my relief I could see her breathing. Upon closer examination I could see white powder smeared on her nose. She looked so peaceful I thought I would wait till Tiny showed up to try and stir her from her slumber. Acting like a true New Yorker, I decided to go on about my business as if the body lying in the middle of the floor was not my problem. I walked back to the office area and saw where the crime was committed. On the desk was a mirror smeared with white powder and a plastic straw, cut in half. There was also an empty bottle of Jack Daniels. As the dutiful assistant, I decided to get rid of the evidence. I walked back to the victim and gently wiped the white substance off her nose, thinking that if anyone were to find her, they would just think she had been up all-night laboring over her photos for the book. I went on to set up the studio for the shoot. I heard the door open.

"Oh shit, oh shit," Tiny said as she ran toward Izzy. Tiny bent over her and began shaking her. "Izzy, get up! Get up! You have a shoot in a couple of hours?" Izzy began to stir.

"I feel like I have been hit by a truck. Where's Queen? He was here a minute ago."

Tiny looked around the studio, thinking she would find Bill Queen but instead she saw me going about my business.

"How long have you been here?" Tiny asked.

"Not too long. I found Izzy on the floor, and she seemed so peaceful. I thought I would let her sleep while I set up the studio. Coffee?"

"Help me get her off the floor and onto the couch," Tiny said, trying to lift Izzy up.

"Not too fast. My head feels like it can explode at any minute," Izzy said, slurring her words. We lifted her off the floor and, with her arms extended on our shoulders, walked her to the couch.

"What happened to Queen? He was here helping choose images for my book."

"When I got here, you were the only one here," I said, placing Izzy on the couch.

Eric Queen was the fashion photographer of the day. His reputation in the business was the bad boy, outwardly gay, flamboyant, and always propped up on drugs. He was the go-to photographer for *Vogue*, *Harpers*, and *Elle*. His reputation was further amplified when a rumor circulated that, in Paris, he had a model toss a baby up in the air for visual impact and then didn't catch the baby on the way down. The Parisian authorities banned him from working in Paris. The incident took a toll because when he got back to New York, he was no longer "the" fashion photographer.

"Izzy, Hoffman is going to be here in about an hour, so you have to pull yourself together," Tiny said, shaking Izzy's shoulders.

"I don't feel good. You have to get a hold of him and call off the shoot." Izzy lay back down on the couch.

"Izzy, I can't. Jahnie will kill you if you bail on this shoot. It is too late to cancel. Just throw some cold water on your face and get it together."

Izzy lay on the couch staring at the tin ceiling. Then suddenly she sat up and said, "I can do this, just let me clean up a bit. What time is he coming?"

"In about an hour. I'll order some coffee and breakfast and you go clean yourself up," Tiny said in a gentle and hopeful voice.

There was a sigh of relief from Tiny. I straightened up the photos on the floor and turned on the strobe lights and fine-tuned the portrait lighting. The door buzzed and I jumped up thinking it was Hoffman. When

I touched the intercom button to ask who it was, it turned out to be our breakfast order. "I'll buzz you in," I said.

I set up the food on the table and the three of us sat quietly drinking our coffee and eating. Izzy still looked wasted but at least she was sitting up.

"We're all set up, Izzy. Like Kodak said, all you have to do is press the button," I said smiling. She looked at me, irritated, looked over to the set up and looked back at me. "It's going to be a short session."

The intercom buzzed and I jumped out of my seat. "I'll get it." I ran to the door and pressed the button. "Hello," I said excitedly.

"Is this the Teivel photo studio?" a woman's voice said.

"Yes, it is. May I help you?"

"We are here for a photo shoot. Can you buzz us in?"

"Of course. We are on the third floor. Turn right off the elevator, we're the second door on the left." I buzzed them in and ran back to Izzy and Tiny. "It's showtime!" I said.

The front door opened and in walked Dustin Hoffman and his entourage. His PR person introduced herself to me and Tiny and then introduced Mr. Hoffman.

"Where's Izzy? I haven't seen her in about a year," Hoffman said.

We all looked back and watched Izzy walk toward us. It wasn't a pretty sight. As she got closer, she raised her arms and head as if she were praising Jesus in a Southern Baptist Church.

"Oh Dustin, it's been a long, long night. I didn't get to sleep till about 5 this morning and I am exhausted. I have been up all night working on my book and it is driving me insane. We must reschedule the shoot for another time. I just can't do this now."

There was dead silence in the room, and we all looked at each other, holding our breaths, waiting for Hoffman to respond. "Izzy, can we have a talk? Let's go back to your office area, OK?" Hoffman said in a very paternal voice.

"OK," Izzy said, and she led Hoffman to the back of the studio.

His entourage, Tiny, and I stood around nervously for what seemed forever, till Hoffman and Izzy walked back toward us arm and arm. Hoffman broke the silence. "Based on the evidence of what Izzy just told me, we are going to do this shoot another day. My agent will contact your publisher and they will work something out. But before we leave, I would like to tell a joke. What do you call a dinosaur that never gives up?" We all shrugged our shoulders. "Try and try and try-asaurus." He turned around and, with his people, walked out the door.

Tiny looked at Izzy and me and said, "Well, that didn't go as bad as I thought it would. Izzy, what did you tell him?"

"That I had a stomach virus and felt like shit." Izzy walked back to the couch to lie down.

"Well, I guess we'll reschedule the shoot with Dustin Hoffman," Tiny said.

Just as Tiny got back to her desk the phone rang. I could hear the voice on the other end yelling.

Tiny extended the phone in the direction of Izzy. It was Jahnie and he was furious. When the yelling subsided Tiny brought the phone back to her ear and said, "Izzy isn't here right now but I will tell her." She hung up the phone.

She turned to Izzy. "Jahnie said the Dustin people called him and said that Hoffman will never do another shoot with you again, ever. Jahnie also said he wants you at his office this afternoon and if you don't show up, this may be your last shoot for *Vinyl*. So, I suggest you get yourself together and head up to their offices."

Izzy closed her eyes, curled up in the fetal position and went to sleep.

CHAPTER 23

ALMOST FRIED AT THE Y

I thought that was the end of Izzy's brilliant career and my short and not-so-brilliant assisting career. What I didn't know at the time was that Izzy wanted to be fired.

Izzy woke up as Tiny and I were about to leave for the day.

"What was that all about?" Tiny said to Izzy.

"What was what all about?" Izzy responded, slowly getting up from the couch.

"Your fucking tantrum! Do you know Jahnie is very close to firing you. You need to go up to Vinyl and plead for mercy. Or we will all be out of a job."

Running her fingers through her gnarly hair, Izzy stared at the fuming Tiny.

"We'll be fine. Is Jahnie still in his office? I think it's time I paid him a visit."

Izzy put on her leather motorcycle jacket.

"I'll call and if he still wants to talk, I'll get the limo to take you there," Tiny said, trying to calm herself.

After Izzy left, I turned to Tiny and asked, "What's going on? Will I have a job tomorrow."

"Maybe. It depends on how Izzy plays her cards. I do know she's been offered some other work by *Vanity Way* magazine. They have been on her case to leave *Vinyl* and, as their editor Richard Dock put it, 'become a legitimate photographer.' This is all confidential by the way. You tell anyone and you will be out of a job."

"I thought *Vanity Way* was long gone?" I said.

They are trying a resurrection. Ty Bighauze is investing a lot of money to bring it back and they have been courting Izzy to come work for them. Currently they have Irving Penn, but the word is they want someone younger and au courant to attract the youth market."

"How do you know all this? "I asked.

"I saw the contract they sent over and read between the lines. I think that's why Izzy is tapping into her demons. I mean she's been with *Vinyl* her whole career and now she's asked to be the exclusive photographer of a resurrected magazine that may fail in a year."

"Why would she take that risk?" I asked.

"She's bored shooting Rock and Roll icons. She wants to branch out and photograph the cultural elite. The Zeitgeist. That's my guess," Tiny said.

"So will I still have a job tomorrow?" I asked.

"Maybe. Come back tomorrow and I'll let you know." Tiny smiled.

"Alright, see you tomorrow. I think I'll go drinking tonight," I said.

When I got back to my apartment, Howie was on the couch watching the *Robyn Bird* show. I seemed to startle him, and he jumped up to greet me.

"How was Hoffman? I mean, is he a cool Jew?"

I looked at Howie and his red eyes. "Have you been smoking pot?" I asked.

"Uh, maybe. Why?"

"Well, if I can have a hit or two, I'll tell you all about Hoffman," I said.

"I promise this is the real stuff. I bought it off one my professors," Howie said, pulling a baggy out of his pocket and showing it to me.

I was about to make up some amazing story to impress Howie, but the effects of the pot acted as a truth serum. I think Howie thought the real story was more interesting because he kept rubbing his beard and saying, "Really, wow. Then what happened?" Being the optimist, Howie encouraged me to be positive about my situation. He thought the upcoming date with Izzy's sister was promising. He had his own theories about Izzy's motivations but, then again, he was studying to be a shrink. Emotionally drained and depressed, I headed to bed, not even remembering how I fell asleep.

That weekend I had dinner with Rachel and Derek. I lamented to them how I would probably be looking for a new job and asked Derek if I could do some work again with his company, demolishing pre-war apartments and renovating them to meet current housing standards. In his polite way he said he had the crew he needed but if I really found myself in a bind…

I think they both detected my despair and they said, simultaneously, "You'll be alright, something will come up." Startled by the unison of their voices, we all burst into laughter.

"So, how's Mom and Dad," I said.

"When was the last time you spoke to them?" Rachel asked.

"A couple of weeks. It's been busy. I barely have time to call my friends," I said, feeling a bit guilty.

"They're fine. I spoke to Mom yesterday and she seemed to be in good spirits. She did ask about you and then tried to guilt me into flying to Cleveland for a visit."

"It's OK if you visit your parents," Derek interjected, "but I can't go anywhere until this project is finished."

"I know," Rachel said. "It's just that my mom really wants to meet you."

"I think I should be going," I offered. "I have an early morning and then I have to start searching for another job."

"You don't know if she is going to fire you. Something will work out," Rachel said in her most reassuring voice.

"If you're in a jam, of course you can join my crew," Derek said. "We're about to demolish an apartment and I could use some extra muscle."

"Thanks. You may be hearing from me tomorrow."

I got up from the table, picked up my coat, and hugged my sister goodbye.

"You should go visit Mom and Dad. I'll feel less guilty if you do," I whispered in her ear.

She looked at me.

"Only if you come with me."

"If I'm out of a job tomorrow, I will," I said as the elevator arrived.

The alarm rang much too early. I dragged myself out of bed and dressed. Howie was passed out on the couch with the TV on. I stomped out of the apartment and intentionally slammed the door.

It was a chilly morning and the crowds were on the march. I pushed my way onto the train, feeling blue, thinking how last Friday I could hardly wait to get to the studio and how today I was dreading going into work.

When I arrived, Tiny was at her desk on the phone. I stood by the front door in a distraught trance, slowly scanning the studio to say goodbye to all the things that had become familiar, reassuring myself that something better would come along. The spell was broken when Tiny got off the phone and turned to me saying, "Well, you're going to be a busy boy for the next couple weeks."

"I thought this was my last day?" I responded.

"Why would you think that?"

"You were here last Friday. You saw what happened. Didn't Jahnie sack Izzy?"

"Sort of but Izzy was one step ahead of him and signed a contract with *Vanity Way*. She is now under contract with them, and they will be paying all the bills."

"No shit?"

"It's a sweet contract. She gets one hundred and twenty grand a year, all her expenses paid, including me and you, and for every cover she shoots, an additional ten grand. The kicker is it's not an exclusive contract. She can work with anyone that doesn't conflict with *Vanity*." Tiny placed her index finger over her mouth. "This is confidential and doesn't leave the studio. In fact, don't tell Izzy I told you. She'd fire both of us!"

"I won't even tell my dog."

"You have a dog?" Tiny asked.

"Ah, no. So, what's next?" I asked Tiny.

"She has one shoot this Wednesday at the Y and then you will have to put your traveling shoes on cause you're on your way to LA on Friday and from what I see on the schedule you're going to be there a while."

"The Y?"

"The YWCA. Izzy is photographing the performance artist Lori Anderson. It will be her first for VW, just so ya know, she may be a little crazier than normal," Tiny said.

"Is that possible?" I asked.

"You haven't been here long enough to see the full spectrum.

You're in for a real treat."

"So is Izzy coming in today?" I asked.

"Nope. She probably won't be in till Wednesday. With all the commotion about this transition, I forgot to tell you that her friend Richard Queen died."

"What? What happened?"

"The word is—and this is just a rumor so I'm not sure it's true—he was riding around in his limo Saturday night and picked up a male prostitute. Seems the prostitute stabbed King and took all his coke and money. At least that's what his driver told Tony, who told me."

"That's awful! How is Izzy taking it?"

"Not good. I think she's pretty freaked out about it. She's not answering her phone."

"Is she going to show up on Wednesday?"

"You may have to pry her from her apartment. She'll show up though. She really wants to impress the folks at VW and stick it to Jahnie." Tiny turned back to her desk to answer the phone.

The next two days went fast. I focused on making sure all the gear was working and investigated an underwater housing for the camera, by request from Tiny. My first stop was a family-owned establishment called "Lens and Repro" to look at the options. The place was cluttered with hundreds of cameras and lenses and all types of contraptions for photographers. I learned about the store from an earlier assisting job for the photographer, Peter B. Kaplan. He was famous for his aerial photography of bridges and tall buildings and had me rent a "gyro stabilizer" to steady his camera while shooting out of a helicopter. He was such an abusive human being that I had to restrain myself from pushing him out of the helicopter as a favor to my fellow humanity. His photos were too good to deprive the photo world of his talents.

Perhaps it was all the cameras, the musty smell of old leather cases, or the countless original photos hanging on the walls by such famous photographers as Eisenstaedt, Penn, Avedon, Klein, and Arbus, but I felt like this store was where I belonged. I walked up to a glass counter filled with Leicas and asked Steve, one of the owner's sons, about an underwater housing for a Hasselblad body.

"What is Izzy up too?" Steve said, scratching his chin. "I've never known her to do underwater photography?"

"I don't know. She thinks it might come in handy for a shoot this week," I replied.

"Well, she better use it, since it rents for $700 a day," Steve said.

"Why so much?" I asked.

"It sells for seven grand so it's 10% of the cost. If she rents it for the week, we will count it as five days, so it would only be thirty-five hundred," Steve said grinning.

"Do you mind if I call the studio and double check?"

"Not at all. We have a phone in the back," Steve said, pointing to the back door.

Above the door was an original black and white print of Ralph Gibson's image of a hand holding a gun, from his book *Déjà Vu*.

"Tiny, the rental is $700 a day. Are you sure Izzy wants it?"

"That's what she asked for. Just put it on our account."

"OK. I'll be back in about half an hour."

I hung up the phone and got Steve's attention.

"We'll take it. Just put it on our account."

"Sounds good. I'll show you how it works."

After giving me some instruction, he put the seven-thousand-dollar contraption in a brown paper bag and wished me luck.

I got to the studio early on Wednesday and packed up the gear. Tiny showed up as I was rolling the equipment toward the door.

"I'm ready. When is Izzy coming by?" I asked.

"She'll meet you at the pool at the Y at 10 am."

"The pool? Is that why we rented the underwater casing?"

"I guess. Izzy wants to photograph Lori at the pool. Apparently, she swims every day." "Should I call Tony?"

"You'll have to get a cab. Izzy is meeting Lori for breakfast and wants the limo."

"I'm on it!" I said, just feeling happy to have my job back.

I had never been to a YWCA and was surprised to see how historic it was; *an NYC hidden treasure*, I thought. I pulled the gear out of the back of the cab, tipped the driver, and stacked the five cases on a luggage cart. Entering the old building was like stepping back into time. There was a front desk person, an androgynous-looking woman in her late 40's who stared at me as if I was lost, and I was.

"Can I help you?" she asked in a brusque voice.

"I'm here to take some photos. I'm supposed to meet someone … a short woman wearing tortoise shell glasses."

The desk person replied, "Oh yeah, she was with another woman with short hair who was going swimming. They went to the pool. You're going to need a pass to get in, hun."

"I don't have one. Can I use your phone to make a call?"

"It's your dime!" she replied.

I pulled out a quarter from my back pocket and put it on the desk. I was about to call Tiny when I heard Izzy's voice, "Sam, what are you doing?"

I turned around and saw Izzy in her rumpled khaki pants and oversized denim shirt with the tails out.

"I was trying to find you. I need a pass to get in."

Izzy turned to the woman and said, "He's with me." The woman looked at me bobbing her head up and down and said, "OK. Just make sure he doesn't stray from your side."

"What are we doing?" I asked Izzy.

"I don't know what we are doing but I know what I am doing. I want to take photos of Lori in and out of the pool, so you need to set up a light."

"I brought the underwater housing for the shoot."

Izzy looked in the bag. "That's too bulky. I am probably not going to use it."

"OK," I said, thinking to myself, what a waste of money. We got onto the elevator and went down a flight. When the elevator door opened, the smell of chlorine overwhelmed me and for a moment … it was early Saturday morning at the Jewish Community Center and my mom was dropping me off to go swimming. As Reform Jews, Sundays were for dressing up and going to Temple, but our Saturdays were supposed to be free. As luck would have it, my mother's best friend, Alice, was Orthodox and her family observed the Sabbath starting Friday night and ending Saturday at dusk, so my mother mandated that my sister and I do something appropriately religious on Saturday to purify our souls. Her idea of purification was to drop us off at the JCC where we were required to jump into cold chlorinated water until our skin pruned up.

Izzy looked at me. "Sam. Sam! Hello?"

"Yes?"

"Lori is changing into her suit and should be here soon. I need to be in the pool when I photograph her against the tiled wall. I want you to put a ladder in the middle of the pool and set up the strobe."

I looked at her in panic.

"Izzy, electricity and water don't mix. I could get electrocuted if the synch cord hits the water!"

"You're not going to let that happen," she instructed.

"I don't have a suit!"

"That's not my problem. I'm going to check on Lori in the dressing room and get my suit on and when I get back, I want everything set up and ready to go."

"I need 20 minutes at least." I replied.

Izzy looked at her watch. "OK, 20 minutes, starting now."

I decided to handle the strobe first, realizing I would be wet after I set up the ladder. Of course, the only ladder available was aluminum, which I thought would be a great electrical conductor. Once the strobe light and soft box were in place, I put the strobe pack, containing 800 watts of current, on the rubber paddle boards preventing them from touching the damp floor. I took off my shoes and socks and jumped into the cold chlorinated water. It was the JCC all over again, that same repulsive feeling rushed through my body as I submerged into the water. At least it was the shallow end of the pool.

I had the ladder in the water and the camera back loaded up just when Izzy and Anderson showed up. Anderson was wearing a one-piece red swimsuit and she looked very toned and sharp with her short cropped hair. Izzy wore a silver one-piece suit, very electric. I had never seen Izzy in a bathing suit because she dressed exclusively in oversized wrinkled clothing. She had a very full figure.

"So, what's the plan, Sam?" Izzy asked, looking back at Anderson and smiling.

I cautiously said, "You stand on the metal ladder and I will hand you the camera." I taped the synch chord to the camera body with gaffers to prevent it from falling into the water and killing us all. They both looked at me a little stunned and an awkward silence proceeded until Izzy cleared her throat and with a commanding voice shouted, "OK, let's do this. Lori, I want you to stand against the green tiled wall wearing your swim cap and goggles. We will start there."

Once Izzy was situated on the ladder, I carefully got into the water holding the camera and electrical cord above my head. A flash memory hit me of the B movies I watched as a kid, on the Ghoulardi show. Soldiers wading across the swampy river, rifles above their heads, while the alligators waited patiently on the banks. I carefully handed Izzy the camera.

"Don't drop it!" I advised.

To my relief the shoot went well. Nobody died and Izzy appeared pleased. The whole shoot lasted about 30 minutes and when it was over Izzy looked at me and said, "Nice work. Pack up and we will meet back at the studio to discuss our trip to LA."

It was the first-time Izzy had paid me a compliment. Maybe the death of her friend had softened her up a bit. Maybe, just maybe, she would begin to treat me more as a human being.

I was soaked from my waist down but no matter, the shoot was a success. After getting out the water, the first thing I did was unplug the pack to avoid a tragic ending and a potentially unusual headline in the *New York Post*, "Izzy's Assistant Electrocuted at the Y. Shocking NYC!"

CHAPTER 21

PHOTOGRAPHY CANNOT SHOW TIME

"Cats. Why would anyone make a musical about cats? Tiny, how can I get out of this."

Tiny raised her eyebrows and replied, "First of all, Izzy is looking for a boyfriend for her sister. I don't know why and I don't care to know. But at least you can suck it up for one night and go out with them. I mean Izzy must like you, to go out with you socially. Besides it will make your trip to L.A. a lot more pleasant."

"I don't even like musicals. You think if I do this, Izzy will be easier on me?"

"No, but it's worth a try," Tiny said, turning around to answer the phone. "Yes, he's here. Yes, I'll tell him." Tiny hung up the phone and looked back at me. "Izzy says to meet her at the Winter Garden Theater at 7. I might suggest you get out of those wet clothes and wear something nice tonight. After all, it is opening night."

"I'll do my best. But I don't have any fancy clothes. I can't imagine a musical called Cats will last long on Broadway." I put away the equipment. "By the way, what does her sister look like?"

Tiny shook her head at me. "How the hell do I know? Probably Izzyish."

I dropped off the film on my way to the subway, wondering how this evening was going to play out. When I got back to my apartment Howie was there, sitting at the dining room table, reading a book and davening.

"Howie, I need a favor."

"What do you need," he asked.

"I need to borrow a jacket and tie tonight for a date."

"A date? Mazel tov! Who's the lucky girl?"

"Izzy's sister. It's a blind date. Never met her, but Izzy is trying to set us up."

"Just the two of you?" Howie asked.

"No, Izzy is going to chaperone. Pretty weird."

"I suppose. Why are you dressing up?"

"We're going to see some new musical called Cats."

"No shit! How did you get tickets? I mean this is a Webber musical. It's big!"

"I don't know, Izzy got the tickets. So can I borrow a jacket and tie?"

"Sure, just go into my closet and pick something out. I have to get back to studying. Big exam tomorrow."

"Thanks, Howie. I'll bring you back a program."

"Get two so I can give one to my girlfriend. She's a big Webber fan," Howie said, looking down at his book.

I got dressed. A blue blazer and thin red tie with jeans. I hailed a cab and headed down to Winter Garden. It was packed and I began to panic that I would never find them.

"Sam! Sam!"

I turned around and saw Izzy. Standing next to her was a mini-Izzy, a little more tucked in.

"Sam, Ruth, Ruth, Sam."

I put out my hand. "Pleased to meet you."

"You too," Ruth said, shaking my hand.

We entered the crowded theater. There were paparazzi everywhere. Looking around I started to identify some celebrities smiling at the cameras. I pretended I was also famous. I did see some people staring at Izzy but she ignored their glances and ushered us into the theater.

"Do you live in Manhattan?" I asked Ruth as we sat in our seats.

"No, I'm just visiting from San Francisco."

"What do you do out there?"

"I'm a painter."

"Oh, that's cool. What brings you to New York?"

"My husband and I are separating. Izzy flew me out here to get away from the mess."

I wasn't sure how to respond, but fortunately the lights were dimming which meant we could stop talking. Cats prancing around the stage was something I didn't expect. What was more unexpected was when Ruth put her hand on my thigh and squeezed. I almost jumped out of my seat.

I wasn't sure how the evening was going to end. After the show, Izzy announced that she and her sister were going out to eat. My presence wasn't requested. As we said our goodbyes Ruth gave me a piece a paper, telling me "Here's my number in New York. Give me a call when you have some free time."

"Sure, I would like that," I said.

I couldn't get a cab so I ended up walking home that night, thinking about the consequences of hooking up with Ruth Friday morning. Izzy and I were in the limo heading to JFK. Izzy was in one of her uncomfortably quiet moods. I had learned to just remain quiet until she spoke. I was staring out the window, watching the soft rain trickle down.

"What did you think of my sister? She seemed to like you. Are you going to date her?"

I wasn't sure how to respond. If I said no—which was my inclination—Izzy would most likely be pissed and if I said yes … God, I couldn't imagine the implications. I decided to play it safe. "Maybe."

Silence.

Arriving at the airport, Tony opened Izzy's door and wished us a safe trip. I got out as Izzy sauntered off. "See you in LA," I heard her say.

"Have a good trip, Izzy," I called after her as she disappeared into the terminal. I placed all the luggage on the curbside and slipped the porter a twenty-dollar bill to take it out of my hands.

"Sam, keep an eye on Izzy. She seems a bit off this morning," Tony said as he got back into the limo.

A little off! I thought to myself.

Walking through the terminal, I wondered about the trip. I was kept in the dark about who she was going to photograph in LA. When I got to the gate, Izzy was, per usual, slouched down in a seat.

"What are we going to do in LA?" I asked.

"Take some pictures, eat some sushi," Izzy replied, continuing to stare out the large windows at the planes.

"I mean, who are you going to photograph while we're there?"

"Hockney and maybe a few others."

First class was boarding and Izzy got up. "See you on the left coast," she said.

I watched her board the plane.

I sat for a while and wondered why she was photographing David Hockney. He was not a musician or a famous actor. I had seen his work in Art History class in college. The professor went on and on about his paintings of swimming pools. She also mentioned that he was openly gay and was keen on making that point and explaining his famous painting, "We Two Boys Together Clinging." Why was Izzy photographing a painter? Then I remembered. She was not working for *Vinyl* but for *Vanity Way*. What little I knew about *Vanity Way* was they were a high-brow publication that wrote about the rich and famous for the rich and famous. Hockney fit that category.

LAX with its balmy weather and palm trees triggered a weird flashback for me. I was twelve. My family was on a "big trip" to visit my father's family. "The lucky ones." The ones who survived World War II and found a new life—with wealth—in America. My cousin was an American success story. He escaped the Nazis by living in the woods as a partisan. At some point, he met a French woman refugee who became his wife. After the war they moved to Beverly Hills and he started a manufacturing business. They raised their two children—my second cousins—who spent their youth, as far as I could tell, on the Santa Monica beach.

Now, ten years later, I was back in LA on my own. I thought about calling my cousins but, knowing I couldn't see them, decided not to.

At the Avis counter, I went over a map with the salesperson.

"How do we get to the Chateau Marmont from the airport?" I asked.

The salesperson pulled out a yellow highlighter and traced the route.

I piled all our equipment into a red convertible coupe and we, Izzy and I, headed north on 405 towards Beverly Hills and then onto Sunset Boulevard, to our hotel.

Built in the 1920's as LA's first earthquake-proof apartment building, the Chateau Marmont was modeled after the Chateau D'Amboise in the Loire Valley where Leonardo da Vinci supposedly died. Ever since its advent as a hotel, the Chateau was a place celebrities went to get into trouble—away from fans, the press, and spouses. Just three months earlier, the comedian John Belushi had died here from a speedball injection.

I parked in front of the main door and one of the doormen in a green uniform greeted us.

"Nice to have you back, Ms. Teivel, it's been a while. Would you like me to take your bags?"

Izzy handed him her backpack and said, "Sam will take care of the rest."

"Yes, ma'am. Your rooms are ready. You just need to sign in at the front desk."

I watched the two walk away. Eventually the man in the green uniform returned.

"Excuse me," I said. "Where do I park?"

"Go straight about 50 yards until you see a stone entrance and park in the garage. Do not use the spaces that say 'reserved.'"

"Got it," I said, driving away.

Entering the garage, I saw a narrow parking space and attempted to carefully back into in. Unfortunately, in the process I bumped a car covered in a blue canvas. The noise wasn't much but enough to grab the attention of one of the parking attendants who came running up to the covered car and placed his hand on the spot where I had touched it.

"Is everything alright," I asked nervously.

"I think so. It feels like a small dent, but De Niro's not going to be happy if he notices."

"You mean this is Robert De Niro's car?" I asked.

"Yes, but he is just storing it here while he's traveling. Let's pretend this never happened."

"Sure, that would be fine with me. Thanks." I parked the car and grabbed my bag and headed to the front desk to check in.

"Hi, I'm here with Izzy Teivel. Can you tell me what room I'm staying in?"

The concierge, dressed in a red button-down jacket and wearing a matching red cap, handed me a key and said, "Room 16. Do you need help with your bag?"

"No, I'm fine. But could you tell me where Ms. Teivel is staying?"

He eyed me up and down.

"You must be her new assistant. She always reserves penthouse #29."

"OK, thanks. By the way, what is all the commotion at the pool?" I was looking at a group of oiled women parading around.

"Oh, that's Helmut Newton's crew. He is staging a photo shoot. Best to stay out of his way," he said, picking up the phone and answering, "Chateau Marmont. This is Florence. How can I help you?"

I figured that was my cue to go to my room. I walked through the stone lobby up a flight of marble stairs and down a hallway to my room. It was all so medieval with gray stone walls and thick wooden trim. Right out of an Errol Flynn movie.

When I opened the door to my room, I could see the red light flashing on the phone next to the bed. I dropped my bag and fell onto the bed contemplating whether I should check the message. Lying on my stomach, stretched out, I could feel a release of tension and I closed my eyes. Soft linen, down pillows, and silence. I closed my eyes and fell asleep and dreamt of my stay at my cousins in Beverly Hills. I was floating on an air mattress in their kidney-shaped pool, hearing my cousin Ziggy's voice with his thick European accent asking his wife how long we would be staying and what to do about dinner. I could feel the warm sun on my back.

Awakened by the ring of the phone I was unsure where I was. I reached for the phone and heard Izzy on the other end.

"How come you didn't answer my phone message?"

Before I could say anything, she went on. "No matter. I have some friends stopping by and I don't need you today but be ready tomorrow to go to Hockney's. We'll meet at the lobby at noon for lunch. Have the gear ready. I might decide to shoot tomorrow."

Before I could reply she had hung up the phone. I decided to continue my dream and fell back asleep.

I awoke in the dark and I started to panic that I had forgotten something. I had. I had left the camera case in the car with all the film. I looked at the clock. It was 8 PM. I bolted out of the room and ran to the garage. Everything was as I had left it. The silver case with the cameras and the bag with the film and the Polaroid. Di Nero's car was still there too.

Back in the room I went through my routine of charging the camera, loading the film backs, and cleaning the Polaroid holder. Once settled I started to feel hungry and headed down to the lobby to see what there was to eat. The restaurant was dimly lit and quiet with a few well-dressed customers scattered throughout. An attractive hostess came up to me and asked, "How many?"

"Just me," I said.

After dinner I decided to take a walk. I strolled along a narrow sidewalk down toward Sunset Boulevard. Once on the main street I decided to check out a club I had heard about called Whisky-A-Go-Go. I wasn't sure how far away it was but, being from New York, I didn't mind a long walk. What I did mind was not seeing any other pedestrians on the sidewalk. I started to get spooked and turned around to walk back toward the hotel. A cop car put on its flashers and aimed a spotlight on me. "Stop where you are and keep your hands where we can see them!"

"What's going on?" I said, a bit freaked out.

A policeman got out his car and walked toward me with his hand on his gun. "What are you doing here?" he asked.

"Just taking a walk and looking around. Is that a crime?" I have always had trouble with authority. A friend in college had to restrain me from confronting a cop who wanted to impound my car. It was something my father taught me, something he learned during the war and knew very well, never trust a person in a uniform.

"Can I see your license?" the cop asked.

"License? Why do I need a license to take a walk?" I asked.

"Just show me some form of identification or I may have to take you in."

"Take me in? On what charges?"

I was thinking this was not going well. I decided to bring it down a notch.

"Sir, I was just taking a walk. I am staying at the Château Marmont. I live in New York City and arrived today for a work assignment. If you like, you can escort me back to the hotel and I will show you my license."

He looked me over for a while. Finally, he said, "This is a dangerous part of town. You should head back to your hotel. If you want to go anywhere in this city, you should go by car. Nobody walks around here at night."

I responded compliantly. "I understand, sir. I am heading back to my hotel now. Thank you for your help."

He turned around and got back in his car. I hightailed it back to the Chateau. The cop car shined a spotlight on me as I walked and I decided to do a little dance step for my audience. I was a star in Hollywood.

My phone rang at 8 AM, and I reached over to pick it up.

"We leave in an hour. I'll meet you up front. Have the car packed and ready to go."

Before I could say anything, Izzy hung up. I jumped out of bed, getting my bearings. Fortunately, I had the camera gear ready so all I needed to do was shower, get dressed, get something to eat, and drive the car to the front.

I walked into the parking lot and saw that De Niro's car was still wrapped. *He'll never know*, I thought to myself. I parked the car in front, reclined the driver seat, and soaked in the morning sun. My mind started drifting to the sound of whooshing traffic in the distance. Then I heard the sound of the car door slamming and Izzy's voice. "Let's go!" I sat up. Izzy was sitting next to me, dressed in an oversized white button-down shirt and white jeans.

"Where to?" I asked.

"Hockney's expecting us around 11 at his house. Take Mulholland Drive."

"How do I do that?" I asked.

"I'll direct you," Izzy said, looking at a piece of paper with the directions. "We want to end up on Montcalm Avenue." Perhaps it was being on the west coast or the switch to *Vanity Way*, but something had changed Izzy. She seemed more relaxed. I followed her direction to Hockney's home.

When we arrived, Izzy turned to me and said, "We'll go in together and I will look around. You remain quiet as if you are mute."

"OK," I responded.

Izzy rang the front doorbell and we waited quietly for a minute. Then Izzy started ringing the bell repeatedly until we heard a distant voice with an English accent. "Alright, alright, I'm coming." The door opened and, standing before us, was the preeminent 20th century painter David Hockney, dressed in a white terry cloth bathrobe and wearing a shower cap that covered up his green hair.

"Izzy, so nice to meet you," he said, reaching out his hand to her. "I am running a little late. I had one of those sleepless nights. Felt I was under water," he said chuckling. "Can I get you some tea or coffee? It will be about 20 minutes before I can rinse out this bleach. Who's your friend?" Hockney asked, eyeing me with a smile.

"This is Sam, my assistant."

"Can I get you something, young man?"

Heeding Izzy's advice, I shook my head from side to side.

"Is he mute? "Hockney asked Izzy.

"Sam, you can answer that," Izzy said, looking at me with a scowl.

"No, Mr. Hockney. I am fine. Thank you for asking," I said in my well-mannered voice.

"What a sweet boy, Izzy. If I were you, I would keep him."

"I might," Izzy replied.

"Well, why don't you two sit by the pool while I rinse off and get dressed." Hockney started to walk away.

"David, before you get dressed, I want to take some photos of you now," Izzy said, looking at me and directing me to get some gear.

"Like this! Izzy, you must be kidding. No one sees me like this except my dear friends."

"David, you look great! Just give me a moment to set up a light and get my camera."

Hockney stood there for a while, thinking about Izzy's request. "Under one condition," he finally said.

"What?" said Izzy.

"I photograph you and your assistant photographing me. I am working on a new project incorporating photo collages to tell a story."

"That's fine with me. Just make sure you get my good side."

I quickly set up a light and took some test Polaroids, then handed Izzy the camera. During the entire shoot Hockney was photographing us.

After the session, he showered and got dressed. When he came out of the bathroom, he declared, "I'm hungry. What do you say we all go out for lunch and then off to the desert for more photos?"

"Sure," Izzy replied. "Where do you want to go?"

"One of my favorite restaurants. Carl's Jr. They make the best American burger."

Izzy looked at me and rolled her eyes. "Sounds great! Sam, is all the gear packed up and ready to go?"

"Ready to go," I replied.

I drove while Izzy sat in the front, and Hockney, wearing red pants and a blue jumper, sat in the back. "Where to?" I asked.

"Head east, young man. Head east. We want to get onto Highway 40 going toward the Mojave Desert and just before we get onto 40 there is Carl's Jr., right before the ramp."

"How long does it take to get to the desert?" Izzy asked.

"It is about a 4-hour drive, but worth it!"

Izzy and I turned to each other and raised our eyebrows. I mouthed FOUR HOURS?

"So, Izzy, why do you like taking photographs?" Hockney asked, leaning forward, resting his chin on the front seat.

"It pays the bills and I don't have to make a living working in a coal mine," Izzy replied sarcastically.

"I think it's a waste of time. I mean photography cannot show time and most photographs look the same," Hockney said. I could see him in the rearview mirror. He was looking at me. He winked. "I mean, there are a few good photographs and they are all accidents. I imagine in the near future everyone will be taking photos from a phone or something similar and, as the saying goes, everyone will have their fifteen minutes of fame."

"Didn't Warhol say that?" Izzy asked.

"He wishes. It was actually the European curator Pontus Hulten who said it first. It's just like Andy to fabricate and take credit for all pop culture. As I was saying, photography will never equal painting. It's a mechanical process of recording reality but it reveals nothing about reality."

"So, if you don't think much of photography why do you want to photograph me photographing you?" Izzy said. I could tell she was irritated.

"Well, it will be part of my 'joiner' work."

"Joiner?" Izzy asked.

"It's something I discovered a year ago. It is visually exciting. Like most great photographs, it was found by accident. I was taking Polaroids in my studio and taping them on a board. I could only take sections of the room, so I took lots of images of the room and reassembled them to represent the room. I realized the collection of images revealed a much stronger narrative then a single photograph. It was so exciting I decided to stop painting to spend some time on assembly." As Hockney was telling us about his new passion, he was touching and playing with my curly hair. I looked in the rearview mirror and saw him smiling.

"What about Muybridge? He used photography to reveal time frozen. That is a perfect example of showing time," Izzy said.

"He used the mechanics of photography to stop time but not to reveal time. The way our memory does. All photography shares the same flaw, the lack of time. It goes back to the Camera Obscura. It records a moment of time but sheds no light on time itself. Perspective is so limited with the camera. Picasso and the Cubists toppled the single perspective. That is what I intend to do with 'joiners'—as some of the art critics call my collages."

I shook my head to keep Hockney from playing with my hair. I looked into the rearview mirror. Hockney leaned back into seat.

"Ahhhh that was a great burger. Izzy, you should have tried the vanilla shake. It all makes me a little drowsy. Think about what I said and tell me how a single photo is a better narrative than my joiners. For now, I am going to take a nap."

"David, before you nap, is there a place in the desert you want us to stop?" Izzy asked.

"When you start seeing the snow, we can stop there."

"Snow?" Izzy said.

"OK. Lights out for me. Wake me when we get there."

I looked in the rearview mirror and behind those large round-framed glasses were closed eyes.

I could tell Izzy was getting irritated with the long drive and it didn't help that Hockney basically declared photography not an art form.

Hours later … "Stop, I see some snow," Izzy said.

I pulled over in the middle of what appeared to be nowhere. Izzy turned around and nudged Hockney's arm.

"David, we are here."

Hockney stirred and rubbed his eyes, "Great, that burger really put me to sleep."

He got out, looked around and turned back to us. "This will do," he announced.

"Where should I set up?" I said to Izzy.

"It looks all the same to me. I don't care. Just set up a light facing away from the road," Izzy said.

I jumped out of the car and pulled out the Honda generator that weighed about 70 pounds. I rolled it about 10 yards. Izzy got out of the car as Hockney started taking photos of us with his instamatic camera.

"I'll help you set up," Izzy said, which totally surprised me since she never touched anything but the camera. Startled I said, "Sure, you can set up the light stand while I get a weight to secure it."

I could tell Izzy was posing for Hockney. She struggled with setting up the light stand while I set up the soft box. The wind was picking up and Izzy was getting very dramatic, holding the stand as if she were one of the soldiers raising up the American flag at Iwo Jima, while Hockney kept clicking away. Ironically, he was becoming the photographer and we were becoming his subjects. Izzy decided to step away and talk to Hockney.

"Let me know when the camera backs are loaded. It's going to be a short photo shoot," Izzy said, yelling over the noisy generator.

She was right. Once I set up and handed her the camera, she took twelve exposures and handed the camera back.

"It's a wrap!" she said to Hockney.

"You sure you got everything you need?" Hockney asked.

"I'm sure. Let's get back to the city."

The ride back seemed shorter. It helped that Hockney was telling us stories of his youth in England and his obsessions with painting and pools. Izzy had her eyes closed for most of the ride. We dropped Hockney off at his home. Getting out of the car, he said to us, "Do you know the most money I made on my work was when I sold a tiny book of my sketches of the theater? You may want to try that Izzy."

Izzy was pissed but she managed to wave goodbye. She turned to me, "Let's go get some Sushi."

Izzy insisted on driving. We headed down Ventura Boulevard to Terru Sushi. Izzy was in a bad mood and was silent. I was feeling happy with the warm breeze coming into the car and with the Hockney shoot behind us, not to mention I loved eating sushi. Something I never had growing up in Cleveland.

When we got to the restaurant Izzy decided to go to valet parking.

"May I have the keys to your car, sir?" the valet said extending his hand to Izzy.

She turned and looked at me.

"Sir? Do I look like a man?"

I looked at her and said, "He just saw the leather jacket you're wearing."

"Fuck that!" she said and grabbed the keys out of the ignition tossing them out the window. She got out of the car and walked into the restaurant. I picked up the keys and apologized to the valet for Izzy's behavior. He smiled and said with a smirk, "I think the sushi and sake will calm him down."

I walked into the restaurant. The place was loud and bustling. Izzy was at the sushi bar and I joined her. She had already ordered a couple of warm sakes and was pointing through the glass at the sushi and sashimi on display. As soon as I sat down next to her, five Japanese waiters gathered around us and started singing "Happy Birthday." I looked at Izzy and she said, "It's something they do when they seat a new customer. It's embarrassing but after a couple of drinks it's funny."

I ordered a beer and a "Sexy Roll," a "That's How I Roll," and an "OMG Sushi Roll." Then I ordered three more beers.

The singing waiters continued to belt out "Happy Birthdays" and the crowd went crazy. Izzy scarfed down the sushi and ordered up more sakes. She turned to me, "I make a rule of not fucking my assistants!"

"I know," I said, taking another long hit of beer.

"Do I look like a man to you?" Izzy asked.

"Not at all," I said, trying to sound serious. "I mean, I really think it was the black leather jacket. Remember there are a lot of long-hair Rock and Rollers around here. Plus, you were sitting down in the car and…"

"OK, OK. No more. I get it. I mean Jagger found me sexy enough to fuck so what the fuck!"

"What the fuck," I repeated, raising my beer. We tapped our glasses—beer to sake—and ordered some more sushi. Three hours later the bill arrived. $243. It was well worth it. Izzy was in a good mood. In the parking lot I gave the valet a $20 tip.

"Thank you, gentlemen," he said, and he gave me a nod and a wink.

CHAPTER 25

MADONNA INN
AND THE NAZIS

We checked out of the Chateau and headed north to San Francisco. It was my first time on Highway 1 and I wasn't used to driving the narrow, winding road. One wrong turn and you drop off into the Pacific Ocean. I was concentrating on the hairpin turns and hugging the road when Izzy said, "You know according to Hunter you should speed up around the curbs."

"Wouldn't that be more dangerous?" I asked, holding tighter to the steering wheel, and then added, "Who the fuck is Hunter?"

"Do you ever read?" Izzy barked.

We were uncomfortably silent. After riding in silence for a while, I decided to attempt some light conversation. "By the way, why are we going to San Francisco?"

"First to see my sister, then we are off to photograph some new writer named Walker." Feeling possessed by the tension between us, I started pushing down the foot peddle and speeding up around the curbs. "She lives in some remote cabin in Medicino without water and electricity." Izzy said.

"Is this the same sister you tried to set me up with in NYC?" I said, slowing down as I realized I was losing control.

"This is my other sister; she's married to some dead head," Izzy said sticking her head out the window.

I saw an exit sign for San Luis Obisbo and a small billboard advertising the Madonna Inn. Izzy must have been following my gaze and said, "Turn. We are heading to the Madonna Inn, ever been there?"

"Nope, are we staying the night?" I asked.

"Duhhh," Izzy said in an irritated voice.

We pulled up to the Madonna Inn and I stepped out of the car, looking around in awe. "Is this part of Disneyland?"

"Izzy stopped and looked back at me and said, "In your dreams."

The front entrance was made of large quarry stones that appeared to be imported from some medieval castle in the Black Forest of Germany. The front door was carved oak and the Tudor façade trim was painted pink. We stepped into the lobby, and I felt I had just stepped into a hobbit's home. Large gray boulders, Paul Bunyan furniture, heavy gothic oak woodwork that crowned the floor and ceiling, and beneath my feet, a red floral wall to wall carpet.

"Ms. Teivel, it's good to see you again. Where have you been hiding?" The concierge said.

"It has been a while, Felip, too long. I hope you have my regular room?" Izzy said.

"Did you make a reservation?"

"No, this is a spontaneous stop. The room I prefer is the Swiss Belle, is it available?"

Felip looked down at his guest register and started mumbling some names "Starlight, Sugar and Spice ... ah yes, the Swiss Belle is available but only tonight."

"We're only staying one night, Felip."

"Zo you and your friend will want the room for the night."

Izzy and I looked at each other in mutual horror. "No, that will be my room, what other rooms are available for Sam?"

Felip looked at his list rubbing his chin and said, "I think Zammy will like the Caveman room".

"Sounds perfect, Felip," Izzy looked at me smiling.

Not to give Izzy the last laugh, I blurted, "Does it come with a campfire and a club?"

"Very funny, Zammy." Felip turned to Izzy, "I zink you have a real comedienne traveling with you Izzy, n'est-ce pas?"

True to form, the Caveman room was right out of the Flintstones. The interior decorator must have had some hallucinatory help. Large gray slate panels were joined by white mortar on the floor, and the walls and ceiling were adorned with leopard skins. As I jumped onto the bed, I had a sudden horrifying thought that it may be made from rock. It wasn't. I pulled out the map of Northern California and plotted tomorrow's road trip. Then I called the front desk, asked for a wakeup call at 6 AM and dozed off.

Next thing I heard was a loud knock on the door that I tried to ignore by putting the pillow over my head. I heard some yelling in a language that sounded like German. The door crashed opened, and I sat up in bed, terrified. Three Nazis in full uniform were yelling at me to get out of bed. "What the fuck is going on? Is this some kind of joke?"

"Dis is no joke, get out of zee bed or we will shoot you, Schnell! Schnell!" One of them pointed his pistol at me. I jumped out of bed and threw on my pants as the Nazis kept waving their pistols and ordering me to go into the hallway.

I stumbled into the hallway and saw Izzy being led out by gunpoint. "Izzy! What the fuck is going on?"

She turned around and looked at me and said, "What do you think is going on? They are gathering up all the Jews!"

A Nazi soldier pushed her and yelled, "Nein Reden! No Talking!" They marched us out to the lobby where the other guests were huddled in a tight corner together. Felip, who had just greeted us a couple of hours ago lay dead on the ground, blood staining his perfectly pressed shirt. Like one of the soldiers in Jeff Wall's photograph, Dead Troops Talk, he was strangely smiling as if he had greeted death as a guest.

A tall, thin man with blond hair and blue eyes, dressed as some high-ranking officer, walked into the room and all the soldiers raised their right arms in the air and said "Zieg Heil, Zieg Heil." He walked up to Izzy and said, "Zo you are ze famous celebrity photographer. I have orders to take you to Mein Fuhrer. He vants you to photograph him."

Without a beat, Izzy pointed to me and said, "Not without him." I suddenly felt calm. She really did need me, I wasn't dispensable.

The officer looked at me and said, "Take these two and get rid of the rest!"

They rushed us out of the lobby and, as we departed, I could hear machine guns firing and people screaming. My heart started racing with fear and I yelled, "You can't kill innocent people!" Without thinking I turned to run back but fell to the ground feeling a pain in the back of my head. I was hit by the butt of a rifle.

I lay on the pavement staring at all the black boots when I heard, "Sammy! Get Up! or they will kill you!"

I look up and see Rachel standing over me. "What are you doing here?"

"I came to tell you Dad suffered a heart attack and died. We have to fly back to Cleveland immediately for the funeral." Hearing that news left me inconsolable. I started sobbing and found it hard to breath. Then I heard a church bell ringing repeatedly until I jolted up and found myself alone in a cave, the phone ringing. My wake-up call.

Shaken and sweaty I decided to take a long, hot shower to try and wash away the memory of that vivid nightmare. I needed to call Rachel to make sure everyone was alright. It was 9 AM in NYC. "Hi Rachel, are you awake, is everything O.K.?"

"Of course, Sam, it's been a while, where are you?"

"In a cave somewhere on the coast of California." I replied.

"That sounds strange, is everything alright? I mean we haven't heard from you for a while. Derek and I were getting concerned."

"Everything's fine. I'm on the road with Izzy and we're on our way to San Francisco. I just had a weird dream. I dreamt that you told me Dad died. Is everything OK?"

"Everything is fine on this end," Rachel said, "although I just talked to Mom and she told me that a customer was caught stealing from the store by the on-duty cop, Don. No one was hurt, just shaken. "

"I wish they could move that store into a safer neighborhood, it's too dangerous." I looked at the clock and realized it was late.

"I don't think they will move, after all they're getting old. Hopefully they'll be ready to retire soon." Rachel responded.

I felt a surge of guilt and wondered if I should have stayed in Cleveland and taken over my father's business. That dreamed triggered something inside me, a remorse for not being the dutiful son. "I better get going, I have to prep, and Izzy is probably looking for me. Nice hearing your voice Rachel. Give my love to Derek. When I get back to NYC, let's go out." I said in an upbeat voice.

"That would be great! Call me when you get back, and, when you get a chance, call Mom and Dad. I am sure they would love to hear from you."

"Bye, talk to you soon." I said hanging up the phone.

When I walked into the lobby, I was happy to see Felip behind the counter, very much alive, writing in his ledger. "Good morning, Felip!" I said cheerfully, "Have you seen Izzy?"

CHAPTER 26

THE OTHER SISTER

She kept at me, telling me to speed up around the curves. Was it a death wish? To keep her at bay, I would accelerate on the hairpin, hugging the steep embankment and then slow down as we lurched to the left, hovering over the ocean. We arrived, miraculously, in San Francisco at dusk, with Izzy trying to remember how to get to her sister's house.

I had a flashback to the classic car chase in the movie *Bullet*, where Steve McQueen speeds through the hills and valleys of San Francisco's famous roller coaster roads, flying over steep hills and screeching tires at every turn. Like McQueen, I was making snap decisions on the route because Izzy was lost.

Finally, she recognized the street and ordered me to make an abrupt left turn. We pulled up in front of a rainbow-colored row house on a steep incline. I cranked the emergency brake.

Happy to finally land, I turned to Izzy and asked, "Where are we?" Izzy looked at me as if I was from Mars and responded in a nostalgic tone, "This is where my sister lives, it's called Russian Hill. I went to school just down the road at the Institute."

Izzy slowly got out of the car and walked up the steps to the front door. "Izzy! You made it!" a woman called out. She looked like a West Coast version of Izzy. "Have … him," pointing at me, "park in the garage, it will be safer. Come on in, I made some of Mama's famous chicken soup for dinner." As Izzy disappeared into the house, the red and blue garage door mysteriously opened.

I pulled the car into the narrow garage and saw the words, "Casey Jones You Better Watch Your Speed: Enter at Your Own Risk" emblazoned in yellow/green, fluorescent paint that was illuminated by a black light-bulb above a rainbow-colored doorframe. Seemed to be the way in. When I opened the door, the ether of incense and sounds of the Grateful Dead permeated the mud room. A flashback to the '60's.

I heard Izzy shout, "We are in the kitchen." I walked down the narrow hallway and entered the kitchen/ceramic studio/music center. An old potbelly stove painted cobalt blue was stacked with pots and pans covering all the burners. It appeared to be more of a storage shelf. I continued walking toward the voices, squeezing through the chaos and trying not to knock anything over. Finally I found the eating nook where Izzy and her sister were sitting and talking. I cleared my throat to get their attention. Eventually Izzy looked up at me, "This is my other sister Barbara. We will be staying here tonight, so get the luggage out of the car."

I turned to Barbara and said, "Nice to meet you."

"Is this the guy you set up Ruth with? "Barbara said, turning to Izzy.

"Sort of, I don't think it worked out," she looked at me with a scowl.

"I'll go get the luggage," I said and turned around, heading back to the garage.

To my relief, the evening was uneventful. Barbara, a ceramic artist, worked out of her home, specifically the kitchen. A progressive Jewish woman.

At dinner, the road trip caught up with me and I found myself almost falling asleep in the soup. Not wanting to appear lame, I looked at the sisters and said, "I am sure you two have to a lot to catch up on so I'm heading to bed." A waterbed to be more precise—*how perfect*, I thought.

The last time I slept in a waterbed was my senior year in college. I lived off-campus in a three-story home, Richardsonian Romanesque. Eight male students and one female student inhabited what we liked to call Tilly's Love Palace. My friend, Martin, rented out the waterbed for "special occasions." Feeling restless, I created swooshing sounds by rolling back and forth, imagining myself somewhere in the Mediterranean Sea. I could hear Izzy and Barbara chatting and the laughing getting louder with each passing minute.

Being a natural voyeur (aren't all photographers), I lay quietly trying to listen to their conversation, hoping to gain some insight into Izzy's inner world. Their conversation lulled me to sleep, sailing the deep blue sea.

The calm waters turned torrent and my nightmare returned. I was standing at the stern watching my father swim for his life with sharks in pursuit. I began screaming at him to swim faster, fearful that I would lose him forever before I ever got to know him.

Awakened by laughter, I open my eyes to see Izzy and Barbara laughing at me, rocking the waterbed. "What the…" I said.

"Wake up, we have to go. We have a long way to drive," Izzy said.

"Ok, let me get dressed, and I'll be ready," I said, a bit irritated.

They left the room giggling like two schoolgirls who had just played a prank. I literally rolled out of bed, got dressed, and packed up my stuff. Barbara and Izzy were at the kitchen table drawing lines of coke. "It's a bit early for that, isn't it?" I said.

"You'll need something for the road," Barbara responded.

"I'm good, just some black tea and I'm set."

Izzy ignored us and placed a short plastic straw up her right nostril, snorting the white powder. She sniffled a bit and then drew another line with her left nostril. "I'm ready, let's get moving." She was jazzed up.

"You know, Sam, you should give our sister another chance," Barbara said, looking my way. "I mean Izzy and I feel like you are part of our family. It's not often Izzy feels that way about any of her assistants."

I looked at her and shrugged, trying to appear nonchalant, "Thanks, I'll think it over."

I want to give you one of my pieces before you go," Barbara said, handing me a large ceramic bowl.

I smiled, genuinely surprised. "Not to be ungrateful, but that would be hard to carry on the plane."

Barbara laughed and said, "How silly of me, let me give you a smaller piece." She scanned her shelves and reached for a salmon-glazed coffee cup. "You can have your morning tea in this."

"Thanks Barbara, I will cherish it." I took the cup and carefully placed it in my backpack.

"Let's go, I want to get there before dark," Izzy said anxiously. We said our goodbyes and began our road trip adventure, headed north.

CHAPTER 27

THE COLOR PURPLE

It was a beautiful California morning as we drove north along Highway 101. I could smell the warm, salty air, with the arc of the Golden Gate bridge in my rearview mirror. After the coke wore off, Izzy fell sound asleep. I was tempted to stop in Santa Rosa and get something to eat, but I didn't want to disturb Izzy's peaceful slumber and my blissful drive. I pushed on for a couple more hours before my stomach started grumbling so loud that it woke up Izzy.

"Where are we?" Izzy asked in a mumbled voice, stretching her arms up in the air.

"The Redwood Forest," I replied.

"To the Gulf Stream Waters," she responded in tempo.

Ignoring her response and not taking the bait to sing the next verse, I said, "How far is that?"

"You don't know that song? Where were you born?" Izzy said in her, how dumb are you, voice.

"Very funny," I said. "Can we stop and get something to eat? I'm starving. The Cherry Creek rest stop is in about five miles, according to that sign."

"I suppose, we can get directions to her cabin. It's off Branscomb Road, west of here," Izzy said, looking at her notebook.

We pulled off the highway into a very small town. "Look, there's a Carl's Jr.," I said enthusiastically, "Home of David Hockney." I could see Izzy was still fuming about Hockney.

She looked up from her notebook to glare at me. "Do you see that diner next to the gas station? We'll go there." The exterior of the diner was painted cucumber green which made sense because it was called "The Pickle Diner."

The screen door to the diner made a creaking sound like you hear in a horror movie just as the knife-wielding psycho enters the room. Izzy let the door slam shut with a loud Bang! The waitress sitting behind the counter barely noticed. Glancing up from her romance novel, she said, "You can sit anywhere, hon," and went back to her book.

The place was just about empty. There was an elderly couple sitting in a booth, in time for the early bird special, and an obese man in tan Carhart overalls sitting at the counter, eating a large stack of pancakes. Izzy walked to the furthest booth from the door, away from the other customers. As we both sat down, a young waitress appeared out of nowhere with menus in hand. She looked like Veronica from the Archie Comics books but without privilege. "Can I get you some coffee?" She handed us the laminated one-page menu.

In unison, we said "Yes."

"You're not from around here, are ya?" the waitress said.

Before I could respond, Izzy jumped in and said, "I'm visiting my cousins in Branscomb. How far are we from Branscomb?

"Well, you continue on SR 1 till you get to Laytonville and head West. You should be there in a couple of hours. Your cousin lives out in the middle of nowhere!" the waitress said in delightfully sarcastic voice.

"I guess we're all living out in the middle of nowhere," I responded.

Sensing Izzy's irritation and my misplaced existential response, the waitress abruptly asked, "So what can I get you, hon?"

I jumped in and said, "I'll have your fish and chips with extra tartar."

"Good choice, it's one of my favorites. The cod is fresh, not frozen," the waitress said smiling at me.

"I'll have the huevo rancheros and some cottage fries," Izzy said.

"Man, I'm hungry," I said. "So, what do we know about Alice Walker?"

"You don't know about her book that just came out?" Izzy said, a bit irritated, in keeping with her general mood.

"No, what's it called?"

The Color Purple.

"Is it any good?" I asked naively.

"It's good, so good that it is being censored in the south and there are rumors of the rights being sold to make a movie.

"Sounds impressive. Is that why Alice lives in the middle of nowhere? To hide out from her critics?" I said thinking it was a funny thing to say.

"How the fuck should I know? You can ask her when you see her," Izzy said as our coffee cups were placed in unison on the table. The waitress turned to me and winked, mouthing, "Someone got up on the wrong side of the bed." I smiled and nodded as she turned to Izzy and said, "Your food will be coming right up, ma'am." We ate in silence. The fish and chips were first-rate. Feeling satiated and bit over-caffeinated, I paid the bill and placed the receipt in the envelope.

We resumed, driving up the road as it turned from black tar to gravel. We passed through Laytonville and headed south to Branscomb. I continued on the gravel road, occasionally crossing over cattle guards, wondering when the suspension on the car would crack. "We turn right on "No Return Road," Izzy shouted.

"Where is that?" I asked, gripping the steering wheel tightly and preparing for the worst.

"I don't know, just keep looking." After about a half hour of driving on washboard roads, I saw a small green sign, No Return Road. How accurate, I thought and turned right. It was late afternoon but due to the density of the surrounding forest, it seemed like dusk. I started driving up a mountain pass, crossing a couple of hairpin switchbacks, eventually arriving in a clearing. "That's it," Izzy says, pointing to a one-room cabin, "It's a bit remote."

"No kidding," I responded. As we approached the cabin, a dog started barking. *Déjà vu*, I thought.

A Black woman stepped out, wearing blue jeans and an untucked flannel shirt. "Don't mind him, he barks at everyone, sort of breaks the silence and freaks out the chickens." She greeted us with a big smile. "Glad you could make it; it's not an easy journey. You must be Izzy," she said extending her hand for a formal handshake. "Who is this?" she said, looking at me.

"I'm Sam, her assistant. It's a pleasure to meet you," I responded in my formal voice.

"The pleasure is all mine," she said. "I don't get many visitors, just how I like it. I'll put on some hot water for tea. The outhouse is behind the chicken coop. Full disclosure, I don't have electricity."

"Rustic," Izzy said, then she looked at me, "Set up an outdoor light with a soft box and the generator in that direction. And load up the film backs, I want to shoot at dusk."

"Will do," I said like a good soldier.

"Will you be joining us for tea, Sam? "

"A little later, I hope."

As they walked into the cabin, I looked around at the beautiful landscape ... taking in the surroundings, smelling the sweet mountain air, and listening to the sounds of nature. A few minutes later, I snapped out my mental haze and, as if the autopilot switched on, began setting up the light and loading the film backs. Then I sat on a tree stump and waited, imagining myself as Rodin's Thinker, fist under my chin. A cabin, far away from civilization, an ideal place to think, imagine, and write books. A place to escape from the madness of the egos and the competitive fervor that speed the pulse and create a city of insomnia. This place, in the middle of nowhere, was ideal to heal emotional wounds and make sense of senseless acts of violence and abuse, a place to feel safe, to feel peace, far from the maddening crowds.

"Are we set?" Izzy asked, abruptly ending my reverie.

I jumped up, looked over my shoulder and said, "Ready when you are."

I handed Izzy the camera as she continued talking to Alice. The conversation between Izzy and Alice became sparse and turned into a few directorial comments by Izzy. A few minutes later she announced, "We're done." Izzy handed me the camera, "We'll leave as soon as you pack up." I watched as she walked back to the cabin with Alice.

It was dusk and quiet again. I thought to myself, "That was a short session." As I packed up the gear and looked around at the serene landscape, I imagined my father, all 87 pounds of him, hiding behind a tree, trying to become invisible, keeping one step ahead of the Nazis. I imagined Poland 1939, the woods full of Jews running, not knowing where to turn, trying to survive the terror of Hitler's soldiers. My father was one of them. I lost track of my thoughts; the peaceful surroundings shifted in a morbid direction and I found myself in a faraway place and time. As a second-generation survivor of the Holocaust, I never directly experienced the horrors that my father witnessed; yet, I can never feel at peace in an apparently safe place. Somehow, I have inherited my father's memories without even knowing the details. "Bang! Bang!" Suddenly gunshots rang in the air. I nearly jumped out of skin and spun around, expecting Nazi soldiers.

Alice approached me to say goodbye, "You look scared, Sam, is everything OK? It's not always quiet up here, my neighbor in the next lot likes to hunt at dusk but don't worry, he's harmless." I caught my breath and walked up to her, reaching out to shake her hand. She took hold of my hand with both her hands and looked me in the eye. "We all have pain and conflict inside us. I write about it to make sense out something I can't comprehend and try to soften the hurt. I hope you can find a way to reconcile yours."

I was bewildered and stumbled, saying only, "Thank you. Thank you." As I walked away, I wondered if she was reading my thoughts, did the expression on my face give me away? How did she know? Is she an empath?

On the drive down the mountain pass, I started telling Izzy what happened and how Alice understood me. I was still shaken. Izzy started laughing. "We were talking and she asked about you. I guess she's always looking for new characters for her novels. So, I told her you were conflicted about your sexual identity and thinking of getting a sex change." Izzy started laughing.

"What? Why would you even think that?" I asked incredulously.

I sank back into my seat, thought about it for a while, and faked a laugh. So much for mindreading. But I still felt Alice knew something … I looked at Izzy and began to wonder what I was doing with my life.

CHAPTER 28

THE PIONEER OF NEW JOURNALISM

When we got back to LA, we checked into Chateau Marmont. I was sure DeNiro would be in the lobby ready to confront me about the dent in his car, ready to go Travis Bickle on my sorry ass. At least I would go down reciting the classic line You talkin' to me? To my relief, according to the valet, DeNiro was out working on some comedy movie.

This was a one-night stay. In the morning, I packed up the gear and Izzy and I were off to the airport. We looked up at the overhead schedule of departures to check the gate. "Oh Shit! Our plane doesn't leave for another two hours. I hate staying at the airport. Let's go back to town and see a movie," Izzy declared.

"Izzy, let's just hang out at the airport so we don't miss our flight," knowing instinctively that Izzy would ignore my sensible suggestion. On cue, she turned to me and said, "Come on, let's get a cab and see a movie. I have to check out an up-and-coming actor for another assignment." We left the airport only to circle back and book another flight.

Lift off. It felt good to be back home. The travel was getting to me and I was beginning to question my sanity when I heard from Tiny that Izzy's next assignment was in my backyard, Brooklyn. Izzy would be photographing Norman Mailer. Not bad. After a big adventure, I always felt a little low but I told myself, if I didn't want change, I would have stayed in Cleveland.

My roommate was asleep on the couch, the TV on and dishes piled in the sink. I decided to ignore this depressing entry and tiptoed into my room. I found my copy of Mailer's *The Executioner's Song*, recently purchased at the Strand, and began to read. I had bought the book on my way home from the studio, just in case there was an opportunity to ask Mailer a question without Izzy reprimanding me. I remembered the headlines about the convicted murderer Gary Gilmore. Mailer managed to keep me awake with his compelling interviews of Gilmore, who decided to choose death by firing squad, or as Gilmore was quoted in the book, "A good death." *I mean is it noble or just plain crazy?*

I dozed off, waking up to morning sun streaming through my soiled Manhattan windows. I cracked open the sliding window and stuck my head out, looking down the 19 stories and scanning the busy streets. I remembered the ant farm I had when I was 8, watching the flow of traffic and people heading south and north. The random sounds of the city blurred into a sort of symphony—buses accelerating, taxis honking, police sirens, raw material for an unwritten symphony of urban living—something that might have inspired Charles Ives. Another day in the city.

I walked out to the living room and found Howie still on the couch, but this time awake and watching the morning news. Surprised, he sat up and said in his high-pitched Long Island voice, "When did you get in?"

"Last night. You were sound asleep."

"I have exams coming up. I fell asleep studying. So how was your trip? How long are you here for?"

Not wanting to go into detail I responded with a vague nod, "It was good, but I have to head down to the studio. Izzy is going to photograph Norman Mailer today."

"Norman Mailer! Wow he's one of my favorite writers. Can you get me his autograph?" Howie slumped back into the couch.

"I'll try, but don't count on it. Chances are I'll be on mute during the session."

11 AM

When I got to the studio, as usual Tiny was on the phone. "I know, I know, uh-uh, no she'll be there, I know, not sure, ok, I will call you." Hanging up the phone, Tiny turned to me and said, "She's missing again."

This is getting old. "Does she know she has a shoot this afternoon?" I asked, trying not to sound irritated.

"I don't know, she's not answering her phone and the photo editor is freaking out about the Mailer shoot."

Do you want me to go to her apartment?" I said, beginning to lose my cool. Suddenly we heard the sound of the door opening—Izzy.

Tiny turned to me and whispered, "Looks like she's been up all night."

"Looks like someone didn't get any sleep," I said sarcastically.

"Fuck you, I need to lie down," Izzy mumbled as she threw her lanky body onto the couch. "Hold my calls till noon and just tell those parasites I'm at a doctor's appointment or something." Inaudible sounds came out of her moving mouth as she threw a blanket over her head and turned her body to face the back of the couch.

"Good thing the shoot is not until 2. You better get the gear together just in case she wakes up early." We both looked at her for a while as she jostled the blanket over her head folding herself into the fetal position. Tiny got on the phone and said, "She's here and will be ready to head out to Brooklyn for the shoot this afternoon … me too."

1 PM

I packed up the limo and Izzy slumbered into the car. We drove across the Brooklyn Bridge to Brooklyn Heights.

My first trip to the Heights was with Rachel, she wanted to introduce me to a boyfriend, now a friend, who was a graphic designer at Pushpin Studios and worked with the famous Milton Glazer. The first thing he told me was that I should shave off my beard because it looked Hassidic, then realizing this to be offensive he added, "You have a great chin, you should show if off." When I didn't say anything, he pointed to a brownstone on Montague Street and said, "That's where Dylan lives." Good recovery.

The limo stopped in front of a classic brownstone just off the Brooklyn Promenade. Izzy had fallen asleep. I examined her, long hair across her face like cobwebs, open corner of her mouth and heavy breathing, the way my father used to snore when he settled into his Barcalounger after a 12-hour workday.

I suddenly thought, what's this about? She is rich, famous, talented, and has a pretty good life. My father, on the other hand, witnessed mass murder, almost starved to death, lost everything, and had to start over in a new country, learn a new language, with no money and memories of terror. I started to shut down, again wondering what am I doing with my life? Time to meet Mailer.

"Izzy! Izzy! We're here," I said.

She turned her head toward me and said, "Where?"

"MAILER'S; we are at MAILER'S home, in Brooklyn, he is expecting us ... Now!!!"

"Holy shit! Why didn't you wake me earlier?" She growled at me, "How do I look?"

"Great!!!" I lied.

"Get the gear and wait here. I'll go first and get back to you once I know what I'm doing."

"Sounds like a plan," I said sarcastically. Izzy looked at me as if she wasn't sure how to reply.

"No, come in without the gear and don't say anything." She put her forefinger over my lips. We got out of the limo and she climbed the steps to the front door as if ascending the last meter of Mt. Everest. I stayed one step behind.

She buzzed the intercom and I heard a gruff voice, "On my way." A few minutes later a white-haired elderly man came to the front door. He had a kind face and piercing blue eyes. He reminded me of the actor Spencer Tracy in the movie *The Old Man and the Sea.*

"Come in and bring your friend," Mailer said, looking at me with a smile. We walked up the steep stairway into an open loft area. The first thing I saw was a giant portrait of Marylyn Monroe at the top of the staircase, probably taken by the photographer, Bert Stern. Turning, I scanned the room. On every wall there were floor-to-ceiling bookshelves. Large lead-paned windows faced the East River. It was raining lightly and the sound of the soft rain against the window was comforting. Near the window was a desk piled with note papers and a black Smith and Corona typewriter with a blank sheet of paper in the platen roller.

"Can I get you and your friend some coffee or something?" Mailer said, breaking the silence.

"No, we're fine." Izzy said looking at me. "Sam, why don't you go sit in the car for a while till I call you. Set up a strobe light on the Promenade where I want to shoot."

"It's raining," I responded curtly.

"Keep it all dry till we come down!"

Feeling a bit put out, I got up the nerve and turned to Mailer, extending my hand, "Nice to meet you, Mr. Mailer."

"Nice to meet you too," Mailer said with a cordial smile.

"Actually, my name is Sam, Sam Cohen," I said.

"In that case, nice to meet you, Sam Cohen." I felt his soft hand tighten and hold mine in a formal handshake.

I could tell Izzy was pissed. Sweet revenge, I thought as I headed downstairs to prepare for another experiment of combining electricity and water.

"Where's the boss lady?" Tony asked, flicking a cigarette into a puddle.

"She wants some alone time with Mailer, while I set up a light."

"In this rain? You got balls, Sam!" Tony said incredulously.

"Yep! That is what the lady wants. Do you have any plastic bags or tarps?" I asked.

"I have a plastic tarp in the back and some extra rubber floor mats."

"Great, that should keep me from being electrocuted. I'll be right back; I'm going to look around and scout a location."

"Sounds good, I'll just be here, eating my lunch, alone, again."

I walked down the street toward the Brooklyn Promenade. The rain had lightened up and was turning into mist. *Manhattan is always prettier in the rain*, I thought. It washes away the accumulated filth of the millions of people that roam the streets every day. Looking south in the direction of the East River, I noticed the twin towers peeking through the mist. The southern tip of Manhattan was shrouded in clouds. To the north was the majestic Brooklyn Bridge. It was one of the bridges I climbed when assisting that crazy photographer, Peter B. Kaplan. Now the sun was trying to break through the clouds, creating sparkles of light on the arched metal railing and sparkles in the water.

The question was whether to set up the strobe light, north or south. I decided, on this overcast day, it didn't really matter. I went back to the limo; Tony was still eating and looking at the *Daily News*.

"Can you open the trunk so I can get some gear out?" I said.

"Sure, one sec." Tony placed his half-eaten sandwich on the paper, rubbed his fingers on his black pants, and jumped out of the car.

"I just need the camera case to load some backs for now and will let you know when I need the rest. I loaded up the film backs and secured everything in the camera case. "One more time, Tony." I said. He opened the trunk and pulled out the plastic and rubber mats. The rain had just about stopped, and I was feeling optimistic. I put down the rubber mats preventing an electrical mishap and placed the strobe pack and generator. I secured the light with a 20-pound sandbag and connected all the cords, setting up the tripod and placing the Hasselblad securely on top. As if by rote, I took some light readings, shot a polaroid, and waited the longest 30 seconds in a photographer's life, then peeled the Polaroid and took a look—not bad, not bad at all.

I kept checking, thinking Izzy would be out soon. I would just have to wait. I couldn't leave the equipment for fear it may be stolen or blown by the wind into the river. I waited. I looked out into the East River and wondered why my father didn't enter through Ellis Island like most immigrants after the War. He told me he had cousins in Boston, so that is where he landed. I was never able to find out who they were. He eventually moved to Cleveland, where he really did have cousins who helped him find housing and some direction. According to my mom, my dad had $50 in his pocket and just the clothes on his back, barely speaking a word of English. The great American dream, an immigrant who makes good. I would think about that when I was feeling sorry for myself and choke up, wondering if it really was my responsibility to carry on my father's hard-earned dream and run the damn sporting goods store.

"You ready?" Izzy shouted from a distance. It startled me for a moment and then I snapped into my work mode.

"Whenever you are," I responded.

"Good, let's get started." She looked at me, a little puzzled, and then looked at where I had placed the light. I handed her the camera without missing a beat, not giving her a chance to change a thing. She looked through the camera and scanned the area.

"Where do you want me to stand? "Mailer said. He was wearing a wrinkled dark blue windbreaker and faded jeans. He looked even more like Hemingway's Santiago, played by Spencer Tracy, but without the yellow Fisherman's Raincoat.

"Stand near the railing," Izzy directed him. It started to rain lightly. I took a deep breath and hoped I had secured and covered the strobe light. Memories of the Laurie Anderson shoot. Izzy took a polaroid and handed it to me. I put it under my arm to keep it dry and warm and painstakingly waited 30 seconds and pulled. "One minute Norm, and we can start shooting," Izzy said. She looked at me telepathically, saying "This better work!" I pulled the polaroid and handed her the positive. She looked at it intensely, while I hold my breath. "OK, let's shoot, before the rain washes everything into the East River." I let out a sigh of relief and handed her a film back. She took 24 images and called it a wrap. "Pack it up and I will meet you back at the car," Izzy called to me. She turned to Mailer, "Let's get out of this rain."

I felt a little nervous that Izzy shot only 24 images. I was sure she would want to shoot some interiors. After I packed up, I rang the doorbell to see what was next. Izzy and Mailer greeted me. Izzy looked at me from head to toe and said, "Thank you, Norm, for your time and let's stay in touch." Izzy turned to me and said, "Let's go!"

"Bye, Mr. Mailer," I said shuffling down the steps. Tony jumped out of the limo and opened the door for Izzy. I got in the other side. We drove back to Manhattan in silence. When we arrived, Izzy told me to unpack, run the film to the lab, and go home.

When I stepped into the studio, Tina shouted in a cheery voice, "How'd it go?"

"Wet and brief." I replied.

"Where's Izzy?" Tiny said.

"Not sure, she stayed in the limo while I unpacked and took off."

"Shit! I hope she doesn't disappear. You have another shoot tomorrow and then fly to Florida the next day to shoot Singer."

"A singer?" I asked.

"Not a singer, Isaac B. Singer, the writer. The magazine is doing a spread on famous Jewish writers. I guess they figured since Izzy is Jewish it was a good fit."

"Who is she photographing tomorrow?" I asked.

"Elie Wiesel," Tina said. "He's on the Upper East Side and the shoot is scheduled for 3 PM, SHARP!" She emphasized the word SHARP.

"That's pretty heavy," I said.

"Heavy?" Tina questioned.

"Both are from the "old country" like my dad and Wiesel is a concentration camp survivor, like my dad."

Tina raised her eyebrows and said, "No shit, well then, you'll have plenty to talk about."

CHAPTER 29

A DARK NIGHT

For Sam,

Shalom, Shalom.

Elie Wiesel

When I was 12, I read Ellie Wiesel's book *Night* in one afternoon. In *Night* every human feeling is broken down, every value destroyed. *"Here there are no fathers, no brothers, no friends,"* a kapo tells him. *"Everyone lives and dies for himself alone."*

My father was asked to testify in Germany to recognize the SS officer he hadn't seen in over 35 years. The officer, I later learned, would sit in a chair in the middle of the night and face hundreds of Jews standing in line. Each person would step forward to the officer and he would shout, "Auch Das Recht!" or "Nacht links!" Those who went to the left were sent to the gas chamber. My father was 28 years old at the time.

I didn't sleep well that night. I kept thinking I could have stayed in Cleveland to help my parents run the store, developed deeper relationships with the people in our community, lived a comfortable life. Young, ambitious, and clueless, I had struck out on a path that had taken me far away from all that I knew.

My mind was in a fog. I didn't remember my routine, the brief conversation I had with Howie or the subway ride to the studio. I was sleepwalking. Tiny jarred me out of my zombie state yelling, "Do you know Izzy has a shoot in 3 hours and never checked in!"

"What!" I responded, trying to be present.

"I haven't heard from her since yesterday. I am getting so fucking tired of this. You better pack the gear and take the limo to her apartment and see if she's there!" Tiny stood abruptly and tossed the rolodex at the couch. "I don't know how long I will be able to stand this shit! She's driving me crazy; the calls never stop, the magazines, publicists, drug dealers keep calling ... I swear I am going to quit this week if she doesn't get her shit together!" I could see tears were running down her cheeks. I walked over and gave her a hug. She wrapped her arms around me and just started bawling. "I can't quit! I need this job to pay my rent. She just drives me crazy."

I tried to comfort her with "it will be alright." My response was something my mom would have said, not really reflecting on how I was feeling and it had the same ill effect on Tiny. She kept crying inconsolably. I felt awkward after a while holding Tiny. We had never been that close physically but it was comforting to me too.

"Tiny, I am not sure how long I can work here, either," I said, whispering into her ear.

Tiny abruptly pushed away from me and said sternly, "You CANNOT leave! I need you ... We need you, at least until Izzy gets her shit together."

"That will never happen, she's a mess and nobody tells her. They just continue to throw accolades at her and give her what she wants. The celebrities dote over her because they want to be on the cover of a magazine, the magazines enable her. They ignore her manic behavior and no one will tell her truth! She needs help! I don't know how long I can watch her crash and burn!" I was ranting.

Tiny stood quietly, looking at me. Rubbing the tears away, she said in a serious tone, "Look, I need this job, as crazy as it is. You seem to know how to handle Izzy, she sees you as family member. She can get her act together; I have seen it."

"What do you mean she sees me as her family member? Why do people keep saying that? I feel more like her submissive servant or slave! One small mistake and she pounces on me!"

"It's the coke, Izzy is taking too much of it and her moods are all over the place. She's going to get clean." Tiny said.

"How? She's addicted to the stuff; she's starting to get nose bleeds."

"I shouldn't be telling you this and you CANNOT tell anyone. PROMISE!" Tiny demanded.

"Sure, I promise."

"The magazine called yesterday and told me Izzy is checking into the Betty Ford clinic for three weeks to get clean."

"Wow, really? I mean when is this going to happen?"

"Next week. This will be her last assignment for a while," Tiny said. "That's why you need to hang in there, for just one more day."

"What happens to me after today? Is that it for me too?"

"No, your dumbass, it means you will be covering for Izzy while she's gone."

"Wait, you mean taking photos for her?" I said confused and terrified.

"NO, you will just keep going on as if she's still here. We don't want this to get out in the press. So, you CAN'T TELL A SOUL!"

Then it hit me. "You mean I'll get paid for three weeks to just sit around and pretend I am working?"

"Exactly," Tiny said, smiling for the first time that morning.

"Ok, I'll stay, but I want a raise."

"Not likely, but I'll ask Sanjeet. Deal? You'll stick around?" Tiny said extending her hand.

"Deal!" I said.

CHAPTER 30

NIGHT TURNS
INTO DAY

"Good morning, Tony," I said as he pulled up to the studio.

Tony got out of the limo and opened up the trunk. "Where to today, Sam?"

"We have to drag Izzy out of bed and get her to the Upper East Side," I said as we piled the cases into the trunk.

"I heard she's no longer imbibing," Tony said as he opened the passenger door.

"Word travels fast. I hope you're right."

We arrived at Izzy's apartment and, sitting in the lobby, was Izzy. She was staring down at the floor. "Izzy," I said.

She looked up. "Let's go." I was trying to act like this was normal and when I saw Tony, I gave him the thumbs up.

The ride to Wiesel's apartment was quiet. I looked out the window as we drove through Central Park. I had never experienced a normal day in the two years I worked with Izzy. There was always some drama, conflict, or despair. It was a strange feeling that morning; I kept thinking Izzy would lash out, that she was coiled ready to strike, but there was nothing, it was like she had a lobotomy.

When we got to the location, Izzy told me to unload and wait in the lobby, as usual. I was excited to meet Wiesel. Ever since I read by his novel *Night* straight through in one sitting, without so much as a bathroom break, I wondered about him. How he was able to express the horrors he witnessed in the concentration camps with all the emotional layers and complexities a person encounters when faced with mortality at every moment. It was a conversation I wanted to have. He spoke for my father.

I sat in the lobby, my mind racing, wondering when Izzy would come down. I felt awkward and conspicuous in this ornate lobby with all the photography equipment stacked next to me. People walked by and stared. I sat quietly, inwardly tense, and waited. Izzy finally arrived and told me to bring up the gear. The plan was to go for one shot in his library. "I'll meet you up there and try not to speak." Izzy said, placing her finger up to her lips.

She's still the same, I thought to myself. But I felt I had to say something, to connect with Wiesel, tell him about my father and fill in the blanks. I knew if I spoke, it would be the end of my job assisting Izzy. Maybe that was a good thing.

When I got to the front door with all the gear, I knocked. It was Elie Wiesel who opened the door and he extended his hand to mine. I reached for his hand, and we shook. He placed his other hand on mine and said in his thick accent, "Come on in, Izzy told me about you."

I was stunned and skeptical. I stepped in and dragged all the gear behind me. Izzy was sitting at the table. "Set up the light in his library," she said as she sipped from her teacup. I set up the light and Izzy positioned Wiesel. He sat on the corner of his desk. Behind him were floor-to-ceiling shelves of books. On his desk was the Talmud and the Torah. He took direction from Izzy and the session ended in about half an hour. "It's a wrap," Izzy said, and they both walked out of the room. I was left to pack it all up. I thought that was the shortest session ever, and uninspiring. I wondered whether the new drug-free Izzy would keep her edge.

I was still hoping to talk to Elie and tell him something about my father, but he was gone. I had missed the moment. My stomach clenched and I had one foot out the door when I heard Wiesel say "Samuel, I have something for you." I turned around and he was standing there, looking at me. He handed me a book. It was *Night*.

I couldn't believe he had given me the book that I had read years before, the book that had left an indelible print on my life, that told my father's story. It was signed on the inside cover.

"Thank you, Mr. Wiesel, thank you so much."

"Samuel, never forget, never forget."

"No, Mr. Wiesel, I never will," I said, and I reached out to shake his hand goodbye.

When we got into the limo, I turned to Izzy and said, "Thank you, Izzy, that meant a lot to me."

"Shut the fuck up and don't tell anyone. Anyway, us Jews have to stick together." She turned toward the window and didn't say another word. I opened the book and looked at the inscription, "To Samuel, Never Forget, Elie Wiesel." I looked out the window and felt my eyes tear up.

I still had the book in my hand when we got back to the studio. Tiny was at the desk and, as Izzy walked in, Tiny turned around and said, "Just got a call, the magazine wants you to do one more Jew for the article."

Izzy plopped down on the couch and "Now who? I mean, how many do they want?"

"Apparently there're a lot that fit the description of Intellectual Jews." Tiny looked down at her notes, "Irving Howe. I mean, really, Irving? How Jewish can you get! OIY." Tiny's inhouse sarcasm about Jewishness always made Izzy smile. We both smiled. Coming out of a very waspy White girl, it seemed a context out of context. We had each other's back.

"When is it?" Izzy asked.

"Tomorrow, another Upper East Side job."

"At least I don't have to unpack the gear," I said. "I'll just run this film to the lab and see you tomorrow."

CHAPTER 31

A CHANGE IN THE WIND

Heading home that night I was feeling light for the first time in a long time. Three weeks without Izzy, getting paid, couldn't have come at a better time. Life with Izzy was getting so bad I was beginning to develop gastric ulcers. When I arrived home, there was a note sitting on the living room table, "Hi Sam, I will be at my girlfriend's for the next week, so enjoy the space. Howie." I literally let out a howl of joy.

Entering my bedroom, I noticed the red light blinking on my answering machine. I hit play, "Hi Sam, this is only your mother. (I mean you would think she would know I knew her voice by now.) Something very exciting is coming up and I thought you would be interested in this special event. Call me when you have a moment. Love Mom." Typical of my mom to create suspense. She couldn't just tell me about the news in her message.

"Hi Mom, is everything okay?" I said, trying to sound blasé.

"Oh yes, everything is fine." Silence….

"Well, you left a message about an event. I was wondering what event you were referring to?" I said a bit irritated.

"Oh, your father is going to be in Washington D.C. for the … let me get this right. Hold on I want to get the letter." I could hear the phone receive drop onto the table and hear her yelling "Oh dear, where did you put that letter?"

"It's on the table, Vhy do you vant to know?" I heard my dad ask.

"I have Sam on the phone and want to tell him about the event."

"Vhy, should he care?" my father said.

"Because he should know too in case he wants to go. So just give me the letter!" Silence. "Hi Sam, are you still there?"

"Where else would I be," I said sharply.

"Good, so listen to this. Dear Mr. Cohen, you are invited to the American Gathering of the Holocaust Survivors in Washington D.C., from July 3rd to the 6th. "Isn't that exciting?" My mom said.

"So, is Dad going?" I asked.

"Sure, he is going, and I want you to join him." I was silent for what seemed forever. "Sam, Sam are you still there?"

"Yes, I'm here, but that's next week! I'm not sure I can make it with work and all."

"It would mean so much to your father if you were with him. Plus, I would feel good if you could keep an eye on him. I mean, it's been a while since you saw him, and he is not as young as he used to be. He gets confused sometimes."

"What you mean he GETS confused?" I asked.

"You know, losing things, going the wrong direction, the usual stuff that drives me crazy," my mom said.

"Can I think about it, or at least ask my boss to see if I can take off?" I said.

"Of course, honey, but remember this is next week. It would make your father so happy if you were with him. I mean this is a big deal, he may meet some of the other survivors from his hometown," she said, speaking in her pleading voice.

"That would be interesting. I tell you what, when I go into the studio tomorrow, I'll ask my boss. We are flying down to Florida for a couple of days. I'll get back to you by the end of the week.

"Oh, that would be wonderful if you could go! I will tell your father now."

"Mom don't say anything till I can confirm the time off. I don't want to disappoint Dad, understand?"

"Of course, honey, I understand, I'll wait."

"Okay, I will call tomorrow. Love you, Mom."

"I love you too, Samuel." I held onto the phone receiver and heard her shout, "Oh dear, you'll never guess who's going to join you...." click. Shit, of course she is going to tell him.

CHAPTER 32

THE LAST HURRAH

To Sam
with my greetings and
best wishes
Isaac Bashevis Singer

As soon as I got into the studio, I confronted Tiny and asked her if I could take 3 days off the next week to go to D.C. I expected her to give me a hard time, but her immediate response was "Sure."

The flight down to Miami was thankfully uneventful. Knowing that this was my last trip with Izzy before my three-week paid vacation made me feel impervious to any of her usual antics. I was excited to meet Isaac Beshevis Singer. It brought back a lot of good memories of Temple. His stories were read to us almost every Sunday by Ms. Wallenstein, whose husband was the Cantor of the Temple. I learned the difference between a Schlemiel and Schlimazel. It is the Schlemiel that spills the soup, and it is the Schlimazel the soup lands on. A life lesson for a 10-year-old. "Gimpel the Fool" was one of my favorite stories. Those strange words my father was speaking at home when he was tired or angry were the very words Singer wrote. There were Yiddish words coming out of my father's mouth and only I knew what they meant by watching my mother's reactions. I just thought he was swearing in German. The word my father used the most was schmuck but only after the customer left. I thought it meant, "Take care or see you later." It wasn't until I used the word in Sunday school that I realized it wasn't a nice word. The Rabbi was leaving our class after telling us how important it was to raise money for Israel. As he was leaving, I blurted out "Schmuck!" The Rabbi turned around and looked at me raising his forefinger and waving it to me to come with him.

The usual. We rented a car and drove to the Avalon Hotel in Miami Beach. I stayed in the lobby while Izzy went up to the room to meet Singer. I sat on a red leather backless couch, trying to find a comfortable position. There was a potted palm tree on each end of the couch facing the receptionist desk. I stared at the receptionist as he went about his business, looking busy. The smell of the ocean air was intoxicating, and my mind started to drift. I wished my grandmother would have kept her house in Coral Gables. We used to stay there every winter. I heard my thoughts as if I was thinking out loud, "I wish I could speak Yiddish, I wish I could speak directly to Singer without Izzy pushing me away. I wish…"

Izzy got out of the elevator and walked toward me. "I want to photograph him by his typewriter in the room so bring up some lights. I am also going photograph him at the beach if he's up to it. He's pretty old, so I'm not sure how long he'll last."

"Ok, what room is he in?"

Izzy pulled a crumpled piece of paper out of her pants pocket "Room 512," and walked away. I gathered up the gear cases I needed and left the others with the receptionist, giving him twenty dollars, knowing how much that would irritate Izzy. I wrangled the equipment into the art deco elevator and proceeded to the fifth floor.

I knocked on the door. A young, attractive Eastern European–looking woman with white horn rimmed glasses and a pencil lodged behind her ear opened the door.

"Yes, may I help you?"

"I am with Izzy."

"Oh yes, come on in. I'm Zofia, Mr. Singer's assistant. Do you need help?"

That was a loaded question. "If you could just keep the door open while I bring in the equipment, that would be great. My name is Sam, Sam Cohen." When I told her my last name, she nodded her head as if to say, "You are one of us."

"Of course, oh my, you have lots of boxes," she exclaimed. Once I got in, I looked around. The room was filled with books, uneaten food, and half-filled glasses scattered around the room.

"So, I noticed an accent, where are you from?" I asked.

"I'm from Poland, a small town called Zakopane, do you know?"

"No, I've never been to Poland, but my dad was born there."

"Oh really!" You must tell Mr. Singer, he may even know him," she giggled. Where he is from..."

"Sam! It's time to set up, remember we may not have much time. I was just informed Singer takes a nap at 3," barked Izzy, who had just entered without my seeing her.

I was startled back to work. "Sure, where do you want to start?"

"At his typewriter in the next room."

"Excuse me, Zofia, I need to get to work."

"Of course, I need to straighten up a bit." I looked into her eyes, wondering if her parents also escaped the Holocaust.

As I was setting up, I could see Izzy and Isaac sitting in the kitchen. She towered over this elderly, frail-looking man. He reminded me of my father as he hunched over the table full of papers. He was wearing a powder blue button-down shirt with a dark blue tie and dark blue slacks, black socks, and open-heeled brown slippers. Formally dressed, like my father from the "old country." I could hear his thick accent as he spoke to Izzy, just like my father. Unlike my father, he had crystal blue eyes full of life.

Setting up the lights I looked at the typewriter and did a double take. Instead of the English letters that I used to labor over in journalism school, there were Hebrew-looking letters that I recognized from Temple. Then I looked at the rolled paper coming out of the platen. On it was something that looked like Hebrew but seemed to be more of an ancient secret code.

Zofia must have been watching me because she slowly walked up to me and asked, "Do you read Yiddish?"

"Is that Yiddish, it looks like Hebrew." I whispered so not to disturb Izzy and Isaac in the next room.

"Yes, that is what I type when I transcribe Isaac's writing."

"You transcribe his work?" I said.

"Why, yes, that is why I am here. Although I also keep his coffee hot, straighten up, and manage his wife, Alma." She smiled. "I also translate his work into other languages since he only writes in Yiddish."

He's lucky to have you," I said placing the light stand and turning on the strobe pack.

"I am lucky to be here," she said. "Isaac and my parents got out of Poland just in time. He helped my parents settle in New Jersey and became my surrogate father, when my father died. We were all lucky," she said sighing.

Looking into her big brown eyes, I said sadly, "My father wasn't so lucky, he stayed in Poland and ended up in a concentration camp."

"He was very lucky he survived; so many did not." Zofia responded. I could see Izzy was looking at me anxiously.

"Zofia, I have to get to work." Turning to Izzy, "Ok, Izzy it's time for a polaroid."

"Hand me the camera," Izzy said in an unusually gentle voice.

She started shooting and directing Singer. Eventually, Isaac looked at Izzy and said, "OK I think that's enough, I believe it is time for my nap."

Izzy responded, "So we can continue the session after your nap?"

"I think you have enough, don't you?" This time Singer looked at me and said, "What do you think?"

I didn't know what to say, clearly, he was asking me, not Izzy. I looked at Izzy. Her face was turning red.

"I don't think so, Mr. Singer, what do … what do you think, Izzy?"

Singer blurted, "NO, No, I am asking you, young man!"

"Ok," I looked at Izzy and looked back at Singer. "After your nap, can Izzy shoot some more?" I said.

"Very well, my nap is 2 to 3, then you come back and finish." I could tell Izzy was furious at me, for taking control of the session. I responded with the right answer, so her fury turned to sarcasm.

"I'm going to the beach; you can finish up the shoot."

I was thinking that would be great, this might be my big break in the industry, and responded, "So I will see you back here at 3?" Izzy stormed out of the room, and I thought I should just let her cool down.

CHAPTER 33

A RECURRING DREAM

I turned to Zofia and asked if she wanted to join me downstairs for some coffee. "I stay with Isaac during his naps, but thank you."

"Stay?" I asked her.

"Yes, stay." she replied. I am not sure what that meant but her reply seemed deliberately obtuse.

Not knowing what to do, I decided to head down to the lobby and, like Singer, take a nap. I nestled into an oversized plush chair and closed my eyes. My mind drifted with thoughts of Zofia. I could easily fall in love with her. She was smart, sexy in a librarian fashion, and, most importantly, Jewish. That would make my parents proud. I imagined us getting married in the old Synagogue in Krakow, Poland, built around the 15th century. Rachel, Mom, and Dad, sitting in the front row smiling ear to ear. I look back and to see my bride-to-be walking down aisle, Zofia arm and arm with the famous I. B. Singer. Everything seemed so beautiful and right in the world. Suddenly we hear gunshots outside the Temple and the doors fly open. Sturmabteilung are rushing in. They yell, "Sich Hinlegen! Sich Hinlegen! Jetzt! Jetz!" and start shooting. I wake up alarmed, sweating, and short of breath. It takes me a moment to realize I'm safe, in the lobby of beautiful hotel, far away from my father's nightmare.

I looked at the art deco clock above the receptionist desk. It's almost three o'clock. Shaking off my bad dream I head out toward the beach looking for Izzy. I see her sitting on the sand looking out into the ocean. "It's almost 3, Izzy we should head back to Singer."

She looks up at me and says," I think I am losing it. I could really use some type of drug. I'm just not creative without it. My work is boring and not original."

"Izzy, you're great! Your work is more innovative and original than ever," I say, trying to coax her back.

"Sam, you are a terrible liar." She's right, I am. "I really need to stop, just go away, where no one can find me."

"Izzy let's just get through this shoot and head back to NYC."

I put my arm out to help her up, she grabbed it, and as I pulled her up, she said, "I am such a bitch, why do you put up with me?"

That question stunned me, and I wasn't sure how to respond. "Because you're Izzy Teivel."

We finished up the shoot on the beach. Izzy took Singer and had him sit in a metal lawn chair against a water-rusted concrete wall. It was dusk; the sun was illuminating Singer against the decomposing wall. A background straight from Poland. *She can be brilliant*, I thought. He was wearing dark sunglasses, a white trench coat, and dark blue tennis shoes, holding a black umbrella. Izzy took a Polaroid, handed me the camera, and we waited in silence for 30 seconds. I stared at the legendary writer who eternally captured a vanishing time in Europe. I pulled the Polaroid tab and showed the positive to Izzy. "Ok, let's shoot." It was a photograph for the ages.

CHAPTER 34

RECONCILIATION

Good News! Tiny told me the photo series of Jewish Writers was well received by the editors of *Vanity Way*. Izzy was off to get clean. I was going to do something I never had done in my short life, spend several days alone with my dad.

Taking the Amtrak from NYC to DC gave me time to reflect about working with Izzy and meeting the who's who of writers and artist. Each one of them stayed true to their passions and were singular in their mission. We all make sacrifices, a parent, or an artist. Parents set aside their lives to nurture their children, artists set aside their families to nurture their vision. Both create. I knew from deep inside that I wanted to create. My desire to record life as I see it is perhaps a way to preserve it. Something my father couldn't do. My father. I didn't know what I would learn if anything, but I was off to a conference called The American Gathering of Jewish Holocaust survivors. Could be epic or could be a bust. For once, he would not be at the store, he would not be watching or reading the news, which he did habitually to help him learn English, at least that is what he told us. I secretly thought he was on high alert to see if the Nazis were in America. I couldn't image how the next three days would go. It never dawned on me that my father would be going through his own demons, confronting his past, once again, this time not to prosecute an SS officer but to search for any survivors from his birthplace in Poland that no longer existed.

Once I arrived at the D.C. Amtrak Station, I hailed a cab and headed to Dulles International Airport to greet my dad at the arriving gate, a first for me. We met at the gate in Concourse B. He was dressed in a plaid brown textured tweed suit and matching tie. On his head was a tan braided fedora and he wore a khaki double-breasted trench coat that I guessed he bought for this trip from the Diamonds men's store in Cleveland.

The temperature was in the mid-90's and very humid. My dad, out of synch with the weather, was dressed for an autumn day. I watched him as he walked in my direction. He had a short, uneven gait and he shuffled his glossy black custom-made orthopedic shoes that always looked funny to me. As I approached him, I noticed he was sweating and a bit out of sorts. I hurried my pace and gave him a hug. "Let me take your bag, we'll get a cab to the hotel," I said, not giving him a chance to respond. I suddenly realized I was walking too fast and, when I looked back, my dad was about 30 feet behind me. This was new territory for me.

I walked back to him. "Sorry, you must be tired."

"It's vas a long trip, and I didn't sleep well last night," my dad said.

"No worries, I'll take care of everything." Suddenly I was feeling very parental and proud. We waved to a cab, and we got in. "901 6th Street Northwest, please."

"Dat's the Ampton Inn, I think," responded the cab driver with a heavy accent.

"I think so. Do you mind if I ask where you're from?" This was a habit I developed in NYC with cab drivers. I figured if you're nice to them, they will do their best to get you to your destination safely. But I realized now it was annoying.

"As long as you're not from immigration?"

"No, just curious. You see my father is from Europe and has an accent, so I'm just curious."

I'm from Ethiopia and av' been here for about 6 months," he said.

"Your English is very good, thank you." I sat back in my seat.

"All is good," the driver responded. We stayed silent the rest of the trip.

I looked over at my dad, who was staring out the window. I broke the silence after a while saying, "It's been a while since you've been to D.C.?"

"You know your mutter and I had our honeymoon here," he said looking out the window.

"I forgot, but I wasn't there, so I have a good excuse," thinking that was a dumb thing to say.

When we got to the hotel, we went up to our room. It was odd, since this was the first time in my life I had ever shared a room with my father. Without Rachel or my mom being a distraction, we sat on the two beds, uncomfortably silent. As my father unpacked his suitcase, I decided to start the conversation. "What do you feel like doing the rest of the day?" I asked.

"I'm tired zo I would like to rest, watch some news, and have dinner at zi restaurant down in the lobby," my father responded as he loosened his tie enough to pull it over his head.

"That sounds like a plan," I said with fake enthusiasm. "Do you have the conference schedule for the next three days?" I tested the firmness of the bed. *So-so.*

"It is in my zuitcase, here." He handed me the paper.

"Oh," I said, "You should call Mom and let her know we arrived safely."

"As soon as I'm unpacked."

He called and after talking briefly he handed me the phone, "Your mother wants to talk to you." Every time I heard that phrase throughout my life, I would have a sinking feeling that I had done something wrong. To my relief, my mother was upbeat and overzealous, telling me how great it was that I was with my dad, and this was a real Mitzva, and what a Mensch I was and so on.

I stayed silent throughout her praise and eventually cut her off to tell her that Dad and I were going to the lobby for dinner. "Ok, honey, but do call soon and tell me how you two are getting along?"

"Sure, Mom, do you want to talk to Dad again?"

"No, just tell him I love him and look forward to hearing about his trip. Good night, dear."

"Good night, Mom," I replied.

The evening was quiet. We went to dinner, didn't talk much, and came back to the room. After my dad dressed in his pajamas and lay in bed, he was out like a light. I watched him sleep for a while, vaguely noticed his teeth in a glass of water on the bedside stand. According to my mom, he lost his permanent teeth due to poor nutrition in the camps. He had told me it was because the Nazis had punched his permanent teeth out. I decided it was time to sleep and prepare for the big day. I forgot how loudly my dad snored, so I placed a pillow over my head and counted sheep.

CHAPTER 35

THE BIG EVENT

This was a big deal, the American Gathering of Jewish Holocaust Survivors. It was the first meeting of its kind, and they announced that the draw might be up to 20,000 survivors. President Reagan and Vice President Bush were the keynote speakers, and my new friend Ellie Wiesel was also a speaker. All was to happen at the Capitol Center sports arena, which seated up to 19,000 people for basketball and hockey games, located in Maryland in an eastern suburb of Washington D.C. I had hoped the event would take place closer to the White House, but the size didn't allow that.

When we took a train to the event. I couldn't help but compare my father's ride on this train to reunite with 20,000 other survivors and the train he once told me about that took thousands of Jews to the Death Camps over 40 years ago. It was the end of the war; the Nazi's knew they had lost and asked the Jews to work one more time in the factory. The Jews, according to my father, did not know that status of the war. He got on the train with his brother. My father pleaded with his brother to squeeze through the bars of the moving train, but he was "too scared." My father, who stood five feet five inches tall and weighed about 78 pounds by then, jumped from the train. He later found out that his brother, who was a trained classical violinist and feared the fall from the train would injure his hands, was killed in the final days of the war when the Germans, insanely and systematically, blew up the factory. Now my father was on a train in America to find out what happened to his small town in Poland.

When we arrived at the Capitol Center, there was a long line of people checking in. I could see my father looking anxiously for someone, anyone he might recognize. I snapped some photos of the event and saw a haunting sight, a man in his '80's wearing a camp prison uniform, black and white strips, yellow arm band with the word JUDEN written, and a black and white cap. He was holding a sign "Never Forget, never again."

CHAPTER 36

INSIDE THE CAPITAL CENTER

Once in the cavernous center, my father picked up a packet that described the day's events. I could see him looking around, anxiously, hoping to find someone he had known from his town, in a sea of anxious faces. He wasn't alone. I was experiencing a time warp, listening to the murmur of voices speaking in languages I had heard as a child when my father was on the phone speaking with his relatives or the voice I heard in temple on the High Holy days. Most of the people at the convention were well dressed and wore name tags with the names of the towns they were from before the war. The day's first activity was to go to the table that had the name of your city. This was a heavy way to begin. I was one of taller people in the crowd and led my father to what was called the "Survivor's Village." The gathering was in a large, cavernous room, typical of a sports arena. It was filled with round, white tables, a sign on each table with the names of a country or city in Europe. I was on the lookout for the name Boryslav, Poland. We pushed our way through the crowd, which no one seemed to mind.

People crowded around, walking through the narrow aisles, looking at the small name tags, blurting out cities they recognized. Some wore large signs giving the names of their town. In the center of the room stood a platform and loudspeaker from which survivors could cry out their names and the person they were looking for, often the survivors of a particular concentration camp.

It reminded me of when I was 6 and had gotten lost at the May Company department store in Cleveland. They had a lost and found table for families who got separated. I'd told the concerned-looking woman that I was lost, and she asked what my name was and started to speak into a microphone "We have a lost 6-year-old boy, brown curly hair, brown eyes whose name is Sam looking for his parents. Please come to the fountain and see me, Mable."

The signs were in English, German, and Yiddish. I scanned the room and then I saw it, Boryslav, Poland. "There it is," I said to my father, as if I had found the afikomen at Passover, the ultimate redemption from suffering.

"Not too fast," my father said standing almost paralyzed. I realized he was still processing the potential of seeing someone he knew.

I slowed down the pace and we walked toward the table. Sitting there was a woman in her late '40's with her son. "Oh, my goodness you're from Boryslav," she said, "My husband's from Boryslaw, He's been looking for someone from his hometown all day." To my father's disappointment, the man's name was unfamiliar to him.

When the man finally returned to the table, my father was indifferent to the meeting, and I was surprised at his response. At least the man was from his hometown. They shook hands and introduced their sons. Then they began to talk in what sounded like Yiddish. I took a few photos and we all agreed, many times, how nice it was that they had met.

The second day was more hectic; twice as many people and twice the confusion. When I joined my father at the table, I found him desperately watching every person who walked by. I took some candid photos of him. It felt good to be a photojournalist, to distance my emotions from the breathless anticipation of my father's longing, hiding behind my camera and taking photos. I had stopped taking photos when I started working for Izzy, too much pressure and too little time.

As I was snapping away, I heard "Are you from Boryslaw?"

"Yes." My father replied.

"Me too; what is your name?"

"Jacob Cohen."

"Cohen, Cohen, there were a few Cohens in our village. Jacob, I am Moshe Liebowitz, son of the pharmacy store owner."

"Oh, mein Gott, Gat zal eykh bensthn!" my father started laughing. They hugged and sat down and immediately started speaking in Polish, Yiddish, and, I think, German. I couldn't understand a word.

"Excuse me, excuse MEEE, Dad!" They both looked at me as though I were a from another planet. I asked them to speak English so I could understand. Seeing how upset I was, they both apologized. I was embarrassed but I wanted desperately to know what they were saying. I got what I wanted though their conversation shifted to primarily English but occasionally would slip in a Yiddish or Polish word.

Moshe began to tell me about my father and his family before the war. "Your father had a kind face. He came from a rich family, although we were not poor," he said. "About 40,000 lived in our town, 30,000 were Jews. There was some anti-Semitism, but the Jews, strong in business, had enough power." Moshe's comments started my father recalling the day-to-day life. For me, years of frustration and curiosity started to unravel as I patiently waited to hear, in father's words, about his past. I could feel tears running down my cheeks and I put my camera up to my eye to hide my emotions.

"Moshe's family had their own business. We lived in a nice little town: everybody was happy. They used to come in on Saturday … We used to go to the temple, do you remember, Moshe?"

"Do I remember!"

My father sat back, a dreamy look on his face, and described the fun he had during Purim, not so different from what I experienced as a kid during Purim. For my father, it seemed like a lost memory. "It's from another world," my father said. "I would never imagine, never believe that I would find Moshe here in Washington. After 40 years. 40 years, right!" he said, turning back to Moshe. "Forty years can you imagine..."

Moshe talked about the Rabbi. "The Germans came in and told the Rabbi to clean the streets with the broom. I saw him sweep the street and later went to the Rabbi and asked him. 'What can we do?' and he said, 'God is with you, and He will protect you.' But I look and see that people are being killed." Moshe shook his head in horror and disgust, remembering, and both men sat quietly for a few moments.

I thought to myself, how could anyone have trusted in a God? What did God have to do with it? In Cleveland my father wasn't religious, but he followed the Jewish High Holy days. I'm not sure he believed in a God, but I think he wanted to hold onto some traditions, as a witness and to remind himself that Hitler had truly lost his war against the Jews.

"I was in Vienna after the war, and I worked," my father said. "I was liberated in Ebensee, went to Vienna, and worked for the Americans. I kissed the American tank and said God Bless America when they liberated us." It was strange to hear my father tell this story—I never knew it.

"You never went back to Poland, Jacob?" Moshe asked.

"No, you know why? I was afraid. We were a few boys and they said if we went back to Poland, the Russians would catch us. They would send us to Russia."

"No, that's not true!" Moshe shook his head. "It's propaganda."

My father asked whom he would find in Poland, in Boryslaw.

"A lot, a lot." Moshe said. "After the war, the Jewish people got the power because Russia started socialism in Poland. So, here in America, the FBI is Jewish; the chief of the FBI is Berman—he is Jewish."

"Who is still alive from us?" my father interrupted. "I mean there is you and me and that woman and that man…"

Moshe started talking and they continued, sometimes talking over each other, triggering the memories, and competing to tell me their stories.

My father remembered that his friend had been in the partisan. "I remember because my brother was in the partisan. He would go to the farmers early in the morning and beg for food, take it to the woods and hide. This was the only way you could survive. I escaped the Germans three times," he said proudly. I felt again as I had when I was nine and realized that my father was a hero. But he was no longer a shadow to me. He spoke to me compassionately, as I had always imagined a father and a son spoke.

"Tell him how much we were given to eat," Moshe said.

"Not enough, hardly anything. Thank God I was strong, although my first wife and one of my brothers passed away. He couldn't make it." I felt a wave of anger, knowing that the Nazis had killed my uncles. I tried to imagine him holding a violin, tried to imagine his music. I looked to my father for answers, but he had moved on, his memories fluid and some were pieced together. I saw how death had hardened the memories that surrounded him. "The Germans didn't like it that my brother and I were together, you know, and they separated us. Then I was liberated. By the Americans. It was over. I was alive. My stomach became swollen from all the food they gave us to eat.

Moshe had also shifted back to the end of the war, "We were lucky. My brother and sister survived, although they killed one sister and two brothers." They spoke again about being lucky. I remembered Zofia, Isaac Beshevis Singer's assistant. She also spoke about luck.

My father went on free-associating. He remembered in 1941, seeing Russian planes fly over the town. "The next day the Nazis moved in and put all the Jews in the ghetto. A year later they took us to Kraków-Płaszów, then Mauthausen, Melk, and finally Ebensee.

"I am one of the lucky ones, one of the chosen ones, you know, because God gave me life. That's why I had to come here, to find another one." It amazed me that after all he had gone through, he still spoke about God.

My father expressed his own notions of what caused the war. "Hitler took power because the time was in crisis," he said. "Everything was bad in Germany; no one had work. They opened up the gate to the jails and there was chaos. They told the public that it was because of the Jews that the economy is bad. They blamed the Jews and told the people to kill the Jews and take everything, whatever they could take. That's what started it. My other brother Ignaz had a wife and a child, and I told him to come with me. He was afraid and didn't want to go. The Germans caught them and killed them all. People were all afraid and didn't know where to go. The Germans caught them and killed them. Some believed in life and lived. Those who lost their taste for life went down."

I never considered my father a wise man, but his words struck me as profound and simple. Without knowing it my father had influenced my whole outlook on life. As I was growing up under my mother's wing, my attitudes and reactions to problems were shaped by my father's indomitable spirit for living. An epiphany surfaced in my mind. My obsession for recording the world with my camera was a way to try and recover the loss of family, to trace back and somehow find a link to my father and all who had perished in the concentration camps. Hockney was half-correct. A photo is not the full experience of reality, but it can stop time for a moment and leave an impression for a lifetime.

I heard my father say, "Well, I think we have to go now." He and Moshe had talked for hours and only covered a small part of what I wanted to know. They both stood up, teary-eyed. Moshe Leibovitz kissed my father on the cheek and said, "Bye, Jacob."

As we walked away, my father took a deep breath and smiled. "He kissed me on the cheek," he said.

We stayed an extra day in Washington. It was a quiet time, but the silence was filled with thoughts of what had taken place over the past three days. We parted at the airport with a hug, he returning to Cleveland, I to New York. In my heart I felt we were closer than we had ever been.

A year later I got a call on my answering machine. "Hello, I hope this is Sam Cohen's phone. I have some terrible news, your father passed away last night of a heart attack. Your mother is with us, and she asked me to call. This is your neighbor Ethel Fischer, call when you can, I know your mother would like to hear from you. If this is not Sam Cohen's phone, I apologize." Click!!!

I impassively walked toward the windows in my bedroom and stared blankly into the hazy York City skyline. Emptiness consumed me, time no longer existed. It wasn't until I felt the tears roll down my cheeks that the heavy gravity of the news began to sink in.

He was gone. I was condemned to never hear his voice again, never to learn his secrets, never to tell him how much he meant to me and how much I loved him.

Resolute, I picked up the phone to arrange my flight back to Cleveland.

ACKNOWLEDGMENTS

Book Acknowledgements:

Shout out to my wife Kate, son Makhesh, and daughter Tika who light up my world.

I am deeply grateful to Saudamini Siegrist and Peter Kafer. Without their encouragement, brilliant editing skills, and friendship, I am not sure I would have had the confidence to complete this book. I would also like to thank Ann Gibb and Nonie Haystack for reading the early drafts with an objective critical eye and making insightful suggestions on how to make this book better.

I would like to also thank my friend Abe Frajndlich, a great photographer, and give a big hug to my sister Lisa Shewmon and her husband Dave, whose generous support helped me launch this book.

In Memory of:

I would like to honor the memory of my father, Jack, and my mother, Ruth, who did their best to raise a decent human being, and my sister Melodie who introduced me to the arts and encouraged me to be curious and fearless.

I will never forget my mentors, Mike Fuller and Tommy Weihs, who died way before their time. They trusted a stranger in a strange city, and I believe they still watch over me.

Finally, this book is dedicated to the phantom memory of my extended family who I never got to meet simply because they happen to be Jewish and were born in a place and a time when being Jewish was a crime and punishable by death.

Never Again. Never Again.

ABOUT THE AUTHOR

Steven H. Begleiter is a noted American photographer, born in Cleveland, Ohio. He has published six books on or about photography (Begleiter Books)

This is his first book of fiction.

In addition to his photography business in Denver, Colorado, he is an Adjunct Professor at the Rocky Mountain College of Art and Design.

He has a degree in Photojournalism from Kent State University and has taught at the University of Pennsylvania School of Fine Arts in Philadelphia, PA.

His photography has been published internationally and his artwork is collected and exhibited in galleries.

To learn more, go to https: www.begleiter.com and to learn more about his book *Leaving Cleveland* subscribe to his blog https://leavingcleveland.blog